Dedicated to

Karen L. Merrick
and
Mary Jayne Hunley

CONTENTS

ACKNOWLEDGEMENTS

This book began as a result of an off-hand remark from a fellow member of the National Speakers Association, in which he challenged us to put our material into a book. Many members of our listening audiences also suggested that we should write a book. Before we knew it our conversations began to include talk about "the book." A few months later the manuscript was finally complete.

Anyone who has written a book understands there comes a time when it takes over every spare moment of your life. This book is no exception. So we begin with a special thanks to Chuck's wife, Karen Merrick, for her patience, understanding and support throughout the whole process. Kay's mother, Mary Jayne Hunley, endured hours of listening to various drafts, lending her support and encouragement.

We are indebted to Robert Baker, Richard Berg, Frank Jarc, Dr. Robert Gillogly, Ronald L. Mercer, Richard Merrick, and Sash Spencer, who set aside time from their busy schedules to review the final draft. Their positive reactions to the manuscript coupled with insightful suggestions for revisions were a tremendous gift. To each of you we say a heartfelt, "Thank you."

Finally, we offer appreciation to Del Hozer for his cover design in which he captured the perfect example of a Change Master -- the weathervane!

Explore your higher latitudes....be a Columbus to whole new continents and worlds within you, open new channels, not of trade but of thought.

- Henry David Thoreau

PREFACE

How many people would show up for the Super Bowl if they already knew the final score? Tickets would be hard to sell because the excitement provided by the unfolding strategy, plays, upsets and ultimate victory would be sacrificed. Yet we have found that individuals every day too often are willing to give up the excitement of the journey for assurances of the outcome. When it comes down to me as an individual or my organization, the preference is for the rules to be changed and for a map setting out a predictable path to success be provided.

In a 1994 interview, Stuart Roosa, the late astronaut who flew the Apollo 14 command module *Kitty Hawk* during the third lunar mission in 1971, was asked how his experiences in space had changed his life. Without hesitation he offered this answer: "Space changes nobody. You bring back from space what you bring into space."

During these times of unprecedented change, Roosa's statement takes on new meaning. Tomorrow is invariably different in many ways from today or yesterday. There are no reliable maps, no proven paths that are guaranteed to work exactly the same for the next individual or organization that chooses to follow the current leader or guru. In other words, you take with you from life's experiences what you bring to life.

We have found that once the mysterious shroud surrounding change is blown away, fear is lessened when the principles which allow one to overcome the effects that change has wrought are implemented. While principles do not change, the implementation process is unique to each individual or organization. Thus we have not chosen to write a book that sets out a detailed map, for that would not serve you well when you are in unfamiliar territory or you do not wish to go to the same place as the map is designed to take you. Instead, as we do in our presentations, we have focused on the principles that will allow you to develop your own capabilities for embracing and overcoming the negative effects of change.

Obviously in dealing with a subject like change, there is no way we can take the time or pages necessary to fill in all the gaps. We have consciously chosen to skim along the surface after presenting the principles to encourage you to think in different terms and chart for yourself new worlds within you. Our desire is that you learn something new, gain valuable insights, and find joy in living life incorporating the skills you develop as you become a Change Master.

Charles I. Merrick
Kay Hunley Titchenal
Edmond, Oklahoma
March, 1995

CHANGE MASTER

Charles I. Merrick
Kay Hunley Titchenal

begin (bi-gin′) *v.* To commence; to come into being.

CHAPTER ONE

BEGIN HERE

For over four hundred years societies have been content to live with the law of gravity which states:

> *"two bodies attract each other with a force that is directly proportional to the product of their masses and inversely proportional to the square of the distance between them."*

While we may not have thought daily about the words contained in this scientific law, at the very mention of Sir Isaac Newton, we conjure up a picture in our minds of a man lying under an apple tree and coming to this profound moment of truth that forever altered the world in which we live. Under Newton's law, the world appears orderly and predictable.

Into this ordered and predictable world came Albert Einstein and his theory of relativity which ultimately turned science on its head by bringing in question everything heretofore held sacred.

Enter an era of dramatic change. Enter the need for Change Masters who delight in chaos and who recognize that progress, understanding, regeneration and order will be their gift as masters of change.

There is no longer any doubt that change is occurring at an unprecedented rate in every aspect of our lives. In its aftermath lies uncertainty, fear and chaos for both the individual and the organization. The paradox is that change itself is the creator of life and progress.

Pick up any book today, this one included, and you will find at least one chapter dealing with change. It matters not whether the book is written for the person wanting to know more about business, science, religion or themselves, it must be acknowledged that things have changed. Mastering change is a necessity for those who wish to get the most out of life.

This presents a paradox. The last thing a Change Master expects, or even desires, is a defined blueprint for anything. However, the first thing we as humans seek is a norm by which to conduct ourselves.

We realize that, just as we have come to accept Newton's Law as the only way to understand our universe, we have come to accept reading a book from front to back as the only way to read a book (although in some Eastern cultures this process is reversed). In reality, there are people who read books by beginning in the middle or at the end.

This is a book about change. It is not necessary to read this book according to the norm. Each chapter has been developed to be complete and stand on its own. Begin reading wherever you feel comfortable or wherever your curiosity leads.

Another difference you will find in this book is that the last chapter is unfinished. One reason it is unfinished is that no last chapter on change can be complete as change is forever with us. However, the most important reason the chapter is unfinished is that no one can write what change means to you, except you. As with the other chapters of this book, you may start or finish there. This is *your* book on becoming a Change Master. When the book is complete, the last chapter will contain your personal notes, thoughts, ideas, action plans, bibliography, questions, answers, etc. You will most likely find enjoyment in returning to these pages again and again as you proceed on your exciting journey of mastering change.

A word of caution. One chapter alone does a master make. To assist you in keeping track of your progress, on the next page is a list of chapters that are contained in the book so you may check them off as you read, study and eventually master the material found in each.

Enjoy your journey. Welcome to the exciting world of the future, the world belonging to the Change Master!

CHAPTER CHECKLIST

	Read	Studied	Mastered
Change and The Age of Reckoning	☐	☐	☐
Mastery	☐	☐	☐
Beyond the Familiar	☐	☐	☐
Yesterday, Today and Tomorrow	☐	☐	☐
The Wart Factor	☐	☐	☐
Beyond Paradigm	☐	☐	☐
More Than a Problem	☐	☐	☐
Be a Child	☐	☐	☐
Relationships	☐	☐	☐
My Chapter on Change	☐	☐	☐

Change (chānj) *v.* To be or cause to be different;

CHAPTER TWO

CHANGE AND THE AGE OF RECKONING

Anticipating a game of bobbing for apples, the tub stands ready with a single apple floating on the surface. But let's suppose the game is postponed and that on each subsequent day the number of apples in the tub is doubled until, on the fifteenth day, the tub cannot float any more apples. On what day was the tub half full of apples?

The answer, of course, is the fourteenth day. It took fourteen days to fill the first half of the tub's surface, but only twenty-four hours for the tub to be completely choked with apples.

The Change Master will not miss the significance of the story of the tub of apples, for therein lies an appreciation for the basic attributes of change. Change begins slowly, usually with a single, seemingly insignificant event. It appears deceptively manageable until all at once there is no denying its existence and overwhelming effect as the change moves faster and faster to overtake the familiar.

We wager the above information is not new to the reader. Survey after survey confirms the increased level of stress individuals and corporations alike are experiencing as they seek to handle the ever-changing environment in which they find themselves. What worked effectively yesterday does not work today. What was a successful path for another individual or company in the past does not work when applied to your own situation today. Frustration runs high and, for the majority, success seems elusive.

We don't believe things are that dire; instead we believe this is the optimum time for success. We challenge you to alter the way you view the familiar to see not only the exponential speed at which change occurs, but also to see why change is not something to be feared. At that point you will gain appreciation for the effects of change, where society is today in the repetitive cycle of change, and how you can take advantage of the unique opportunities contained within the uncertainties that surround change. Perhaps then you will understand why we prefer to call this "The Age of Reckoning."

The best place to begin is by taking a look at the history of man's existence on earth. Next we will take a look at specific shifts within the historical overview to bring into focus what is happening today. Finally we will discuss the elements of change and offer suggestions for mastering the skills necessary to overcome its negative effects.

Approximately eight million years ago, humans roamed the earth in small groups, moving from place to place to follow the food supply. Anthropologists tell us these groups of people inhabited a small portion of the earth, primarily in climates that posed the least threat to their well-being. The majority of their waking hours were spent in activities geared toward survival.

Status in these nomadic communities was earned through one's prowess as a hunter and the ability to understand the ways of nature. Though unable to alter nature, out of reverence, awe and acceptance of her natural laws, hunters became more knowledgeable about their environment and improved their ability to roam over ever-increasing areas of the earth.

Assets during this period of mankind's history were two-fold. First was the rudimentary tools developed to assist with hunting and second was the knowledge and ability of the hunter which allowed him to be creative and flexible.

Approximately 10,000 years ago an event that triggered the transition from hunter to farmer occurred with a dramatic change in weather patterns. Suddenly summers were hot and dry and winters were cool and wet. Plants that had survived in earlier times were now undergoing change to adapt to the new environment. The three primary crops -- barley, oats and wheat -- produced larger heads of grain so the seeds could handle the drier periods. This change in climate also led to the demise of larger, predatory animals as plant life in the wilderness became more scarce. There followed a shift in man's ability to find food by hunting animals so he turned to grain as a primary source of food. In a span of approximately 200 years humans were abruptly forced to change their way of life. The old ways of the hunter were no longer effective and the assets and tools of the previous era decreased in value.

After the initial upheaval and a tumultuous period of adjustment, a better lifestyle began to emerge. It was no longer necessary to move from place to place as hunters. Animals were domesticated and plant species were developed. There was time to absorb the change. Nearly six million years after first inhabiting the earth, humans were able to settle in one place. The era of the hunter had come to an end.

Over the next 6,000 years, 200 species of plants and 50 species of animals were domesticated. In 2000 BC the chicken became the last animal to be domesticated. There has been virtually no additional domestication of plants and animals since that time.

As farmers, time was devoted to learning how to manipulate nature for our own purpose by building shelters to keep out cold, pumping water to irrigate land, and learning to preserve vegetables and meat. Farmers retained the attributes of the hunter in regard to respecting the laws of nature, but also sought ways to harness those laws for their own benefit.

The era of the farmer also came to an end. Proof of the era's demise can be found in the fact that the 1990 U.S. census no longer had "farmer" as a category since they made up such an insignificant number of the population.

In 1733, John Kay of Lanchashire, England provided the insignificant event that set the stage for the Industrial Revolution. His invention, the flying shuttle, was a simple device which greatly improved the speed by which cotton could be woven into cloth. It was now possible for one person to weave a double width of cloth.

Three years later, in 1736, Leonhardt Euler, the Swiss physicist, published his *Authentica Mechanica.* Thus, seventy years after Isaac Newton introduced his theories of gravity and ushered in a mechanical view of the universe, there existed a mathematical format based on those theories which would usher in the age of the machines -- the Industrial Revolution.

Within less than 100 years inventions became the norm of the day, creating mechanical devices that would re-define the way goods were produced. Nature was harnessed to provide the power to run factories and transport goods across land and sea.

Assets of this era moved from ownership of land to ownership of factories, business entities and power sources necessary to run machines.

Once again there had been a tremendous upheaval, changing forever the way life was expected to be conducted. The old ways no longer worked and the assets of the previous era had begun to lose their luster. Farming was subjected to the new pressures of the mechanical age as more and more machinery became necessary to make a profitable living. Once again, after the initial shock of the change, there came a period during which a modicum of normalcy returned and a more predictable way of conducting the business of life unfolded.

Two hundred and sixty years later the next insignificant event would take place to alter the history of man. The month was January, the year was 1993, and the insignificant event took place on Wall Street, the center of capitalism. On that date and in that place, the value of the stock of Microsoft, a $2 billion company specializing in information technology, was worth more than the stock of General Motors, a $250 billion company specializing in producing a machine, the automobile. Less than 80 years after Einstein proposed his theories of relativity, the age of quantum physics and information burst upon us.

With the transition into this era, the age of paradox was underway. Some have called it the information age, space age or technological age. We have dubbed it the age of paradox because it truly represents an age that appears to contradict itself.

We expected this new "information age" to bring about more informed decisions because of the ease of generating data. In addition, the new technology would provide leisure time to pursue other interests in life. The paradox is the expectations are in conflict with what appears to be true.

Here's an example. Recently we were in the process of negotiating a complex contract regarding a large business acquisition. It was the norm to discuss changes on the telephone as midnight approached and then fax the material directly from the computer sitting on our desk to the one at the law office over 600 miles away. There the word processors worked overnight to make changes and fax the material back to our computer in time for the 7:00 a.m. conference call to discuss the changes and current status. Working at this pace, with the assistance of the "time saving" technological tools at our disposal, this contract was executed just ten days after the first discussion.

Ironically less than ten years ago a similar incident occurred. The procedure then was to work on the changes, hand it to the word processor in time to have a copy in overnight delivery by 9:00 p.m. whereupon everyone re-grouped to review what happened, said "good night" and went home since there would be no further activity until the 10:00 a.m. delivery of the package the following day. This contract took six weeks to complete despite the fact that "time was of the essence."

Thus the paradox is brought into focus. We indeec have more reliable data, and technology has provided the tools to accomplish tasks faster than ever before. However the leisure time that was to be made available has been consumed by the need to immediately move on to the next project.

Underlying this speed at which events take place is the fact that decisions must be made immediately with the information at hand. There is no luxury of time to sort through data, hold lengthy strategy sessions, and expect a "time out" during the process.

Less than 400 years ago, just before Newton emerged on the backdrop of history, a person could conceivably know about all there was to know in the entire world. Today we are so inundated with information and new practices that the human mind experiences difficulty in sorting through the morass to garner relevant knowledge and relationships. The old ways of doing business no longer apply and time, rather than capital, is becoming the valued asset.

The pattern that emerges from this historical overview is that there is an event, usually overlooked at the time, that sets in motion the onslaught of a major change. From hunter to farmer it was a change in the climate. In the last two shifts it was an idea in the scientific realm, first Newton and then Einstein, that provided the basis for change. There follows a relatively short period of time during which the old rules are no longer effective and for which new rules or standards have yet to be recognized. This is a very chaotic period and, paradoxically, a very creative period.

The speed of change is shown by the graph below depicting the pace at which society has made major shifts, i.e. from hunter to farmer to industrial revolution to paradox. Clearly it has taken far less time to move from one era to another. The nomadic

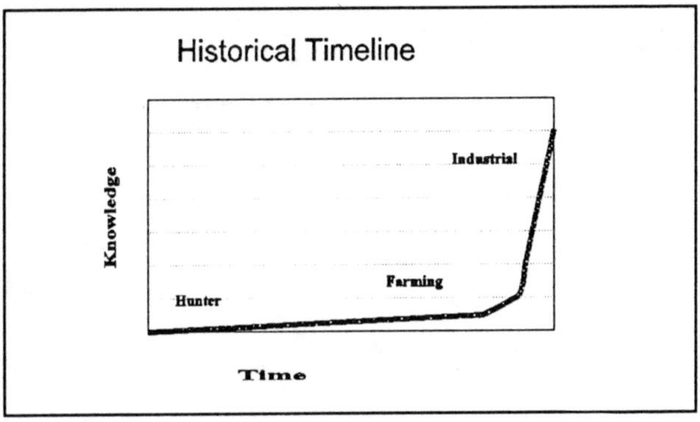

Figure 1

hunter society with its assets grounded in the tools for hunting lasted for millions of years; the farmer with assets of land prevailed for over 6,000 years; the industrial age with factories and capital as assets was replaced in less than 300 years. History illustrates that change does not occur as a straight-line, linear progression, but instead approximates an e-function, or exponential, curve.

Another look at the graph illustrates that as we continue to progress, it is imperative not to fall behind in keeping pace with change because catching up again becomes nearly impossible. The individual or organization who has opted to "rest" has forfeited continual development of knowledge and relationships, becoming the equivalent of a stone-age hunter in a computer-age paradox.

At this point let's change our focus from the birds-eye view of the history of mankind and look at what happens within each of these major shifts. As we moved from the farmer to the industrial era, for example, other shifts are to be found which were surrounded by unprecedented chaos. We are currently engulfed in one such period of chaos, which explains why interest in change is so prevalent. It should be less threatening, however, as we realize that we have experienced these shifts in the past.

Let's delve back to the shift from farming to the Industrial Revolution. During the age of machines, we progressed from horse power to steam power to gas power, each time creating a major shift in how work was done and life was lived.

Prior to agriculture being a mainstay of society, individuals would tend to small plots of land to grow enough food for their own family and animals. As trade routes opened and farming became the basis of society's economy and way of life, farmers turned to horsepower to plant and harvest their corps. A farmer who relied on horses typically farmed about 70 acres and two horses. To keep each horse fed and pastured took seven acres of the farmer's land.

Productivity immediately increased 20% with the advent of the steam engine. Thrashers and tractors fueled by coal and wood driven steam engines enabled the farmer to put the 14 acres previously devoted to sustaining the life of horses into production. Prior to the advent of steam engines, there was a need for large families or hired help to bring in crops. Corn was shucked by hand, weeds pulled by hand and hay stacked by hand. Now there were machines that could do these tasks. Those individuals who understood how to operate and repair the steam powered machinery were now in demand. The middle class, made up of managers of agricultural workers or craftsmen skilled in the art of shoeing horses and mending harnesses, were no longer sought after as the need for their expertise disappeared.

After steam engines came gas powered machines. Machinery became more efficient and there was another upheaval in farming as the small family farm gave way to larger family or corporate farms. Farming was now a business, not a way of life. People who had run smaller farms were disappearing and again there was a great upheaval in the economy of those who farmed the land or who supported the farming

During these transitional times, what people do for a living changes dramatically. People lose their familiar jobs and those who have not continued learning new skills find themselves shoved out of the middle class as the gulf between the poor and rich increases.

We saw the same effects in the industrial age which is now entering the early stages of its demise. When factories were first started in the United States the work force was made up of individuals from all corners of the world, all speaking different languages with little or no education. It was necessary to have a layer of management that could direct the work of the individual laborers, who could speak foreign languages to get the work done. Labor unions were developed to represent the worker in this transaction.

Public education was imposed to develop a work force that could understand a common language, develop rudimentary skills and attain a level of literacy. Middle management and labor unions continued to survive as business was conducted as usual.

With the move from gasoline powered machinery to robots and computer controlled systems, the need for individuals with skills beyond the routine repair of machinery is growing. The individual who has neglected to keep up with the new technology soon discovers it is more and more difficult to find jobs that pay well. This revolution has all the characteristics of the one that took place when the workforce moved from steam powered engines to gasoline powered engines.

In addition, with the emergence of a world market and the need for speed, businesses today are finding that they need to develop direct partnerships between management and employees. The need for a labor union as a third party to negotiate these matters has diminished and middle management is no longer necessary as workers begin to develop their own schedules and methods for getting the work done. The middle class as it currently exists is again being threatened.

Briefly the cycle goes like this: Those individuals who enter the workplace equip themselves with current skills or at best are anxious to learn the new technology. They are at the bottom and are looking up at opportunity. They do not waste their time and energy on learning the old way of doing things. In other words, they become skilled in gas powered machinery, not in steam powered machinery.

Those caught in the middle who have gained the experience and understanding of the current technology usually become complacent as they improve their skills, assuming they have achieved the level of success that guarantees their future. Since their history does not include gas powered machinery, they remain skeptical of its usefulness and, at best, do not see the new technology doing away with the old. As we see from the past, they are soon replaced and their economic level in society is lowered.

The same thing happens to the middle-man in the business realm. For example, Wal☆Mart has demonstrated to the retail industry that the distributor is no longer as necessary as the company became its own distributor.

Meanwhile, those who see the full picture understand that the world is emerging into an ever increasing competitive marketplace requiring massive shifts in the way businesses and lives are conducted. They take the necessary steps to prepare for the shift to new technology and increase their value as they position themselves as a bridge between the past and future. Their value comes when past experience, coupled with expertise in both the old and new technology, creates a level of wisdom.

One lesson that stands out for the Change Master is that the future is for keeps. There is no going back to the present to start over. Therefore, it is imperative that learning and developing the attributes of flexibility and creativity become a priority. It is also important to recognize that we are individually responsible for this activity and cannot wait for our company, government or anyone else to do it for us.

With each upheaval comes opportunity for redefining life and work. Remember when our expectations for the computer or information age was improved wages and increased leisure time? The fact is that take home wages in the United States in 1993 were 21% lower than in 1973. Workers today are putting in 158 more hours per year, roughly equivalent to an extra month. There is less time to do necessary chores. However, new opportunities abound. In an environment where time is a precious commodity, individuals and businesses are looking for someone to take care of their lawns, take care of their children, run their errands, and handle routine tasks. Who would have expected forty years ago that someone could make a living walking dogs for people, addressing holiday greeting cards or acting as a personal shopper.

Earlier we stated that time rather than capital was the valued asset in the new era. An example can be seen in conversations about travel. We used to note that a particular place was so many miles from where we were presently located. Today we measure that distance in time -- one hour or two days. Not only do we measure the distance in time, we plan our itineraries to take the least amount of time to get from one place to the next, often willing to spend more cash to gain the time. Our mobile phones and laptop computers have further guaranteed that we will not be idle during what was otherwise considered unproductive time spent in travel.

History has shown again and again that those individuals or businesses who seize the opportunities presented during these times of upheaval and who recognize the emerging change in assets are those who achieve tremendous success. In fact there are more successful businesses and lifestyles launched during these chaotic times than at any other time in history.

The purpose of this discussion is to point out that there is nothing new under the sun. There are only new ways of doing work and interacting. If you are sitting around waiting for the good old days to return, you have guaranteed your obsolescence. If you are lamenting that things are worse than they have ever been, you are overlooking hidden opportunities that exist in periods of upheaval throughout history.

Another attribute of change occurring today is its effect on systems. Ironically, systems have evolved from being complex to becoming simple while operations, once very simple, have increased in complexity.

There are three illustrations that will assist in understanding this shift to simple systems and complex operations. The first is the shift to simpler systems which rely less on physical machines or materials. Ticketless airline travel is a prime example. As the industry moves to save an estimated $2 billion in costs for materials, printing and handling of tickets, the system is being streamlined. However, the importance of independent decisions of employees in the industry is increased.

The second illustration is the move to on-line computer networks which allows the news to be "read" on screen without need for hard copy. Again, the system has being simplified, but the individual is required to become more flexible by learning new ways, understanding what is and is not available from the networks, and knowing how to seek out necessary and relevant information.

A third illustration can be found in the lights that are placed on Christmas trees and outdoor displays throughout the country during the holiday season. Remember when a string of lights that had one bulb go out meant that all bulbs would not light. It was necessary to spend time testing *each* bulb until the culprit had been isolated and replaced. Today each bulb acts on its own and one can be out without effecting the whole string. In addition, it is possible to "program" the lights to go on and off in various configurations. A string of lights is no longer a simple matter, the operator determines the patterns, the color of the lights and the amount of time each display will last. A simple system, a complicated operation.

Ironically we have another paradox for in many ways we have returned to the age of the hunter where the prowess of the individual is mandatory for survival.

Overall, a balance must be maintained between systems and operations. During the Industrial

Revolution the complicated systems required little skill from the individual. Basically an individual had to know how to turn machines on and off, how to make routine repairs, and how to move output from one place to another. Today, systems are becoming simplified, thus the human factor must be relied on to balance the overall complexity. Individuals must be more flexible, maintain faster communication links and cannot wait for a "boss" to tell them what to do. Our frustration as we move to this new age of paradox or reckoning comes from being overloaded with bureaucracy which thwarts our ability to react quickly as we know we must.

Now as to our explanation of why we call this the Age of Reckoning.

Reckoning in its noun form means to calculate the position of a ship, aircraft, etc. This era of change surrounding a major shift in our history requires that we actively and purposefully take the time to calculate our direction in terms of the present *and* the future.

There are four elements to be considered by those who choose to reckon with change.

The first is that change is occurring faster than ever before. As we have seen from the historical examples, the major shifts in society are taking less time to surface. In our own lifetimes we have seen entire occupations disappear. For example, as a child I remember going to the department store and having an elevator operator at the controls to bring the car to a stop, sometimes making minor adjustments in an attempt to be sure the level of the elevator floor coincided with that of the floor of the building. Today elevators are programmed to do the job on their own at a push of a button and in addition many welcome you aboard while announcing the time, temperature and floor in the process.

The method of conducting our lives has also changed in a short period of time. It is now common knowledge that computers contain the ability to send facsimile messages and the Internet is fast becoming the norm for communicating on a personal and professional level. The latest technology is "smart" in that it can advise us of potential problems. A baby's diaper, currently in the early stages of development, is being designed to advise the parent when the baby is wet. Vehicle tires may soon "tell" you when they are low on air or need to be replaced.

In short, there is no time to relax and drop out of the mainstream or you will be left so far behind it soon becomes impossible to catch up. Return to that exponential curve graph (Figure 1) that correctly depicts the speed of change. As you can see, in the early stages it may be possible to keep up, but as the curve takes off in an almost perpendicular direction from the base the ability to catch up has been compromised. Scientists have shown that with concentrated effort, it is possible to come to within 3% to 4% of the top of the exponential curve. But it is not likely that you will overcome, or become, the leader.

On a personal level, it is much like learning to ride a bicycle. The first person that learns takes all the risks as they achieve the objective. By observing their actions, mistakes and corrections, it is easier for the next person to learn to ride a bicycle. Likewise, even when you are behind the curve, by focusing on the leader and learning from their trailblazing, you can achieve great strides faster than the leader did on his first try. But there comes a point where you have expended too much of your energies and other resources on catching up. In the process you have not had the luxury of learning the nuances of the ascent and have not developed the wherewithal to explore the uncharted territories. You are, therefore, relegated to second place, or worse.

In other words, you may be a great bicycle rider, but

the leader has gone on to racing or doing tricks on the bicycle and mere riding is no longer enough to remain competitive.

By acknowledging the existence of the exponential speed of change and by not viewing it as a terminal disease, the Change Master understands the importance of maintaining expertise in the current technology while reaching out to embrace the new.

The second element in reckoning with change is that we are living at a time of significant change when we will be guaranteed to be surrounded by chaos. A recent event illustrates this chaotic environment and what happens when it is denied. In November 1989 the impossible happened when the wall between East and West Berlin began to fall. There was a tremendous celebration and the expectation was that with the end of the Cold War and freedom from the threat of nuclear war, there would be a reunification of a great city after 44 years of division. Five years later it is obvious that all the expectations have not been met. Families have been brought together and people from the East can now work in the West. But there remains a wall in the mind of the Berlin people who have remained focused on their unpleasant recent *past.* By refusing to venture into the unknown and unfamiliar many East Berliners remain on their side of the city and do not yet call themselves Berliners. People in the West complain about the new taxes required to help rebuild East Berlin. Unemployment has increased and tensions are increasing as well. The wall is down, but the refusal to accept and deal with the real issues of chaos and a break from the norm has, for all practical purposes kept the wall in place.

Refusing to let go of the past and step outside into the chaos that will not go away, dooms you to become a relic of the past.

The third element is that you alone make the choice to participate in the transition to the new. Philip B. Crosby, in his book *Quality is Free* has described this the best as he states:

> *It always makes me wonder when people ask, "what did you study in college?" What difference can it make? People don't do for a living what they learned in college anyway. Management, unless you are in a true professional field such as chemistry or medicine is very much a general knowledge thing. The more information you have about everything...the more you can accomplish.*

Therefore, it is essential to never cease learning. Taking formal learning courses whenever possible is one sure way of learning something. But it is more important to just read and listen. Read everything. Read at least one magazine every day and three or four books a month (on any subject). Dig up several good conversations each week. And don't get hung up on the same routine for recreation. Keep alive and uncommitted.

It is not possible to know what you need to learn. Therefore, you have to constantly seek out new experiences and exposures."

The only way to be a participant in change is to constantly increase your knowledge base.

The fourth and final element is that you can survive only if you are prepared to be an agent of change. You prepare by gaining an understanding of your values. Values are those guiding principles that define your life and character. Unless you clearly understand what is meaningful to you in life, then you are doomed to be tossed about on the winds of change surrendering to others the power to define your status and worth.

Robert Louis Stevenson is quoted as saying:

> *Quiet minds cannot be perplexed or frightened, but go on in fortune or misfortune at their own private pace, like a (wind-up) clock in a thunderstorm.*

When you have grasped the meaning for your own life, your own source of power and peace, then and only then can you become an agent of change. Living in harmony with your values means you will not lose your focus on that which is important. No matter how fast the world is changing around you, you will find yourself increasingly more creative, innovative and willing to seek the opportunities that lie within the chaos surrounding change.

Until one recognizes and masters the effects of change, particularly the speed and amount of change, and consciously makes the decision to choose to move forward, old methods will be inappropriately idolized and remain the norm while the rest of the world is operating under a new set of rules. Ultimately decay sets in and demise soon follows. Those individuals and organizations that remain will have become masters of the important aspect of the speed of change and instead of decaying will find new energy in the process of regeneration.

Mastery (măs′tə-rē) *n.* Attainment of skills, knowledge and ability to overcome

CHAPTER THREE

MASTERY

Mastery. This word is rapidly creeping into our vocabulary and is being applied to every aspect of our lives. The promise held forth is that by sheer determination one can gain absolute control over any subject or concern at hand simply by applying mastery. Naturally, it follows, by achieving mastery, life will be filled with happiness and tranquility. While we will admit there is a kernel of truth in this, we would caution that there is much more to mastery than a quick study of any situation. Mastery takes time, commitment and passion. The reward of achieving mastery is the ability to overcome the negative aspects of change.

Change, whether positive or negative, robs us of control. Psychologists and social scientists have discovered that humans possess an inner drive to attain control over their environment. Given this fact it is not surprising that there is such a strong fear of change. There is nothing inherently wrong with this attitude of seeking to achieve control for there are indeed times, especially during a crisis, when maintaining control over the situation is an absolute necessity for survival. However, when maintaining control over all aspects of life becomes the goal, the end result is stress and disappointment, a far cry from the tranquility and order that was expected.

Humans have long held a fascination with the weather. With the introduction of computers, it appeared that the ability to predict the weather through accurate forecasts would be within reach. However, as late as the 1960's meteorologists were wary of the place of computers in their world and felt forecasting weather was a travesty to the profession. During this same time period some meteorologists and graduate students at the Massachusetts Institute of Technology were beating a path to the office of Edward Lorenz to place their bets on the forecasting prowess of the toy weather machine Lorenz had created. Edward Lorenz had been interested in weather since childhood. He often wondered why, if it was possible for scientists to predict the return of Haley's Comet every seventy-six years and for accurate tide charts to be developed months in advance, then why couldn't the weather be predicted months in advance as well. His toy machine was successful in predicting the weather a few days in advance, but was still unable to predict whether New York City would have sun or rain on a particular day one month away.

Ultimately, and quite by accident, Lorenz discovered what is known in scientific circles today as the Lorenz Attractor, and more popularly as the butterfly effect. Lorenz had reduced his mathematical model for weather into three simple equations which became the basis for his toy weather machine. One day after interrupting the computerized weather toy, Lorenz entered data by hand instead of waiting for the computer to begin the process from the beginning. The result was that while the pattern repeated itself as in the past, the lines on the paper made loops that reversed on themselves, looking like butterfly wings. Figure 3.1 below shows the pattern that was created.

In layman's terms, Lorenz had discovered that the weather in New York could be effected by the flapping of the wings of a butterfly in Hong Kong. The effect of the disruption of the air current by such an insignificant event could impact the weather occurring days later in a place on earth thousands of miles away from the event itself.

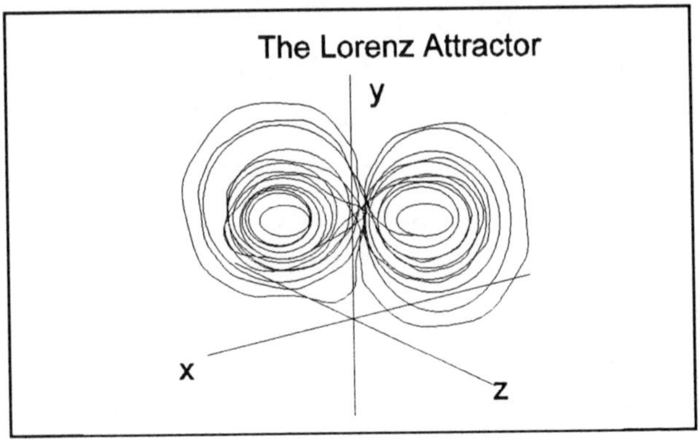

Figure 3.1

Assuming our goal is to attempt to control the weather, it would appear the task at hand is to identify and then modify all interruptions that would have an effect on weather patterns. Just think of all the important events that have been "rained out," or ski vacations planned months in advance that are a disappointment because of lack of snow!

Reality slaps us in the face for at this point of our attempt to gain control in order to successfully control the weather, all interruptions to air currents would have to be regulated. That includes jets taking off and landing in Sydney, screen doors slamming in Nebraska, Big Ben striking in London, the elevator going up the Eiffel Tower or a kite flying along the coast of Japan. It would also include controlling the movements of all of nature's creatures. The ability to anticipate and prevent all those interruptions is mindboggling and an exercise in futility.

In many ways, life is not much different than the weather. Events occurring in our backyard or half a world away can have just as much effect on our daily lives and future as the butterfly in Hong Kong has on the weather in New York City. These events can encompass the crumbling of the Berlin Wall, a stock market crash, introduction of new technology, a newly attained college degree or a promotion at work. The events don't have to be negative. Positive events disrupt our lives and momentarily threaten our control in the same manner as negative events.

Every event described above involves change. After all, change is nothing more than something different from what was expected, something out of the ordinary. Every day we face deviations from expectations without falling to pieces, failing, or experiencing measurable stress.

So why the emphasis on mastering change?

To understand the answer to that question, it is important to acknowledge the *amount* of change that is occurring. Only then does it become clear that attempts to cope with or manage change are as futile as trying to control the weather.

Change is occurring not only with increased rapidity, but on several fronts at the same time, cutting across lines separating generations, industries and leisure activities. In mid-1994 those with a computer and a on-line service, Compu-Serve, were the first to gain access to the rock group, Aerosmith's release of a single from their latest CD. It was several days before the CD from which the single was taken was available in music stores or was played on the airwaves. In many locales it is possible to place your grocery order by computer before you leave for work in the morning and to pick up your order at the drive-through section of the grocery store on your way home at night. It is not uncommon for individuals in their sixties (and older) to be toting a cellular phone on the golf links or in their automobiles. Wash basins at many public restrooms today do not have a means for manually turning on and off the water. An electronic eye senses your presence and regulates the faucets, delivering a stream of water at the proper temperature when needed. Surgery that once required a week's stay in the hospital is now done on an outpatient basis. Desert Storm was beamed into our homes via satellite as it was happening.

In as many, yet less dramatic ways, we encounter change every day. It may be nothing more than a nick while shaving, a water-soaked morning paper, a traffic tie-up on the way to work, an unexpected financial windfall or a presentation that turned out better than expected.

It is not difficult to handle one or perhaps two of these disruptions at a time. Given time to fully assimilate the disruption, the event causes barely discernable stress. However, when events occur one on top of the other, or before there is enough time to absorb the impact of the previous disruption we reach saturation and may even become dysfunctional. Businesses as well as individuals experience the consequences of change. Major changes such as downsizing, re-engineering, pressures from competitors, acquisitions, unexpected growth and major shifts in the marketplace can cause anything from a minor business disruption to complete failure.

Obviously, change is a force that must be acknowledged. There are basically three methods for handling change: coping, managing and mastering. Individuals and businesses commonly choose to cope or manage change. Very seldom is mastery applied. Let's look at each of these methods in more detail.

To "cope" is defined in the dictionary as successfully striving or contending with something. Generally, coping is how one deals with a situation that is expected to improve over time. The inference is that if energy is directed toward maintaining the status quo, the disruption will cease to be of concern. You cope with a headache. You cope with a visit from the in-laws. You cope with a temporary business set-back. You cope with inflation. But what happens when the interruption doesn't go away? What happens when the change that has taken place becomes the new way of doing business? Then coping doesn't work anymore because maintaining status quo requires the application of all available resources, leaving the individual or business reduced to striving and contending, usually not successfully.

Perhaps one of the reasons we tend to rely on coping as a way of handling change is that past experience has shown that many times things appear to return to an acceptable norm. A brief discussion of linear and non-linear systems may be helpful in explaining why this is a viable, but not necessarily profitable, observation.

A linear system is predictable and is based on repetitive formulas. One example of a linear system can be found in retirement planning. To predict the amount of money you will have accumulated from the current date to a specified date in the future, a simple interest rate is usually assumed. By applying an uncomplicated and repetitive formula, a conclusion is easy to reach. The results plotted on a graph will take the form of a straight line. The accumulated monies at any given point in time between the present and a specified date in the future are also predictable points along the line. The graph below illustrates this linear system.

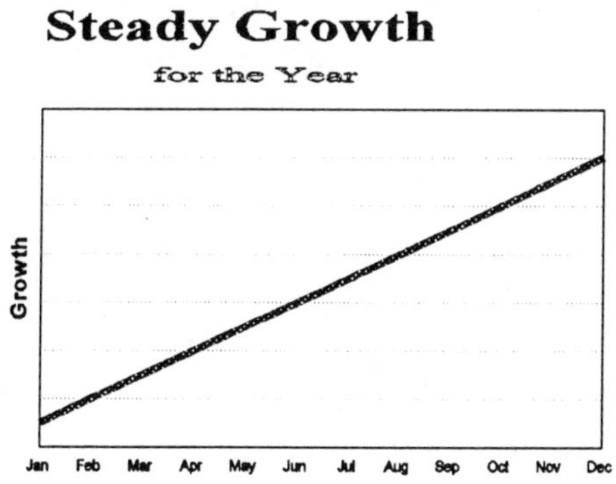

Figure 3.2

A nonlinear system on the other hand, may have unpredictable outcomes. Yet as Lorenz has demonstrated with his toy weather machine, over a period of time a non-linear system tends to display a familiar pattern. The irony is that the repeated pattern, while similar, is not exactly the same. For example, depending upon where you are in the universe, you can predict that hot weather can be expected in July. However, if you were to select a particular place and take the same date in July, say July 4, and look back over the last decade, you will find that no two July 4ths were exactly the same. You may find two years in which the temperatures were the same, but another variable, such as humidity will be different. The pattern of hot weather has repeated itself, but there are subtle differences. These subtle differences can too easily be overlooked if the approach to change is that of coping. As these differences accumulate you will find yourself or your business left behind and unable to contend with the stress.

An example of the effect of accumulated subtle differences can be seen in computer operating environments. Microsoft Corporation is responsible for the Disc Operating System (MS-DOS) used on the majority of computers in the United States. Microsoft is also responsible for the Windows system. Talk to anyone who has moved from using a program in MS-DOS to using the same program in Windows. Invariably they will point out that while there are many similarities, the subtle differences are an initial source of frustration. Screens do not look the same, commands often differ, and the finished product may not appear the same. There are individuals who refuse to move from the current version of their software program electing to cope with the frustrations of interfacing with others who have moved on to new versions. But there comes a point where communication ceases to be effective and diskettes containing needed data can no longer be shared. By not appreciating the subtle changes and mastering the new programs, one is left behind to become obsolete. Catching up is tantamount to starting over. Valuable time and energy has been lost in the process.

Coping is no longer a viable option for the massive change that is taking place in today's environment.

To "manage" is defined in the dictionary as directing, controlling, or making submissive.

There are two aspects about managing that are deceiving when applied to change. First, as can be seen by Lorenz' "butterfly effect" research, there are too many independent variables in too many places outside the parameters of our business or personal life that can, in reality, be controlled and made submissive. Second, control is not an option when it comes to living creatures, and that includes humans.

Imagine the event of a lifetime that has been planned to the most minute detail. The best minds in the organization (family or business) have been put to work on developing the schedule, deciding the site and pulling together the right people to witness such an auspicious occasion. There are no pre-event jitters, just pleasant anticipation of watching the unfolding of the program and basking in the results. For sake of example, let's assume the event is the introduction of the first electric car that has the public lined up to place orders. The pre-event publicity has been in place, anticipation is high, and invitations to the unveiling are coveted. News media have sent their top reporters to witness the break-through in technology which will usher in a major change in personal transportation. As the project manager, you have arrived early, checked into your hotel room and ordered room service. Looking forward to a quiet evening before the "big day" you switch on the television in time to catch the news.

The lead story concerns a daring rescue event in a country that is in a part of the world unfamiliar to you. The rescue is of a small child, the daughter of a well-respected and well-known world dignitary. All programming will be interrupted while live cameras and commentators bring the drama to the world via satellite. The telephone begins to ring. Those invited to the event are cancelling. Major news sources expected at the electric car unveiling are re-assigning reporters leaving your event covered, if at all, by unknowns. Air time may or may not be available in the immediate future depending on the story unfolding half a world away. The focus on an electric car seems less important and certainly less newsworthy since it can be covered at a later date.

How do you control and make submissive those who were invited and now have cancelled, the news media that relegates this history-making event to a secondary story, and how do you recover the momentum caused by the interruption? This is a make-believe story but it happens every day in less dramatic ways in our businesses and personal lives. Sometimes the change creeps up on us, catching us unaware. Sometimes the change, as in a crisis, is rapid and totally unexpected. In truth, there is no guarantee that absolute control is ever possible in the realm of change.

Obviously overlooked in the above example is the manager who has planned ahead and has contingencies in place. While the negative impact may be mitigated as a result of the contingency planning, the fact remains that there has been damage and loss of energy. The final outcome will be dictated by the ability to assimilate and respond to change, not by application of the management roles of directing, controlling and making submissive.

Mastery, on the other hand, goes beyond mere management or repetitious patterns. Mastery is defined as attaining the skills, knowledge and ability to overcome. Mastery is further understood as a consummate skill, that is, a perfect or complete skill. Therefore, mastery doesn't come about by mere practice, but by a combination of passion, experience and continual improvement, whether on a personal or organizational level. Risk taking is the acceptable mode and the resulting accomplishments go beyond mere lessons to attainment of a level of awareness that meets each new challenge with renewed confidence.

You may find yourself asking the following questions: Why won't coping and managing suffice? After all, if things are changing so fast, what difference can it make? Besides, doesn't becoming a master take too much time to be an effective approach to overcome change?

The question to ask is: Why give up making the right decisions and effecting the future positively which can only be achieved through mastery? By applying four simple principles, mastery can be within your grasp.

The first principle is to take full advantage of any training that can be made available to you. Sometimes this is formal education, but just as often can be time spent at a library reading the latest information, or historical information, about a given subject. Perhaps it is a hobby that is pursued or special interest groups that bring additional knowledge or skills. The key is to explore as many items of interest and to gain as much knowledge and skill in various areas as is possible.

The second principle is to take time to reflect on your own life experiences. Often an experience in one area can be applied to another issue or can assist in seeing future trends. Failures lead to future success if the time is taken to understand what has happened and what could have changed the course of events.

The third principle is to embrace risk taking. When thrust into a new environment, thrive on the opportunity to learn and adapt rather than become caught up in fear of the unknown.

The last principle is to be willing to remain flexible and creative. Abandon the "I've always done it this way" approach and explore other avenues and opportunities.

These four principles -- taking advantage of training, applying your unique life experiences and abilities to the situation at hand, embracing risk, and remaining flexible and creative -- is your path to mastery.

A mutual friend, Richard T. Berg, former President of Wilson Foods Corporation, a Fortune 500 Company, tells of a time in 1946 when he found himself as a twenty-one year old officer on a destroyer in the Antarctica. The Commodore of the operating group had been the navigator for Admiral Byrd's first expedition to the South Pole some fifteen years prior to this mission. The destroyer's Captain had not had a ship command at anytime during his career. He had not spent much time at sea. The majority of the Commodore's time during the five-month tour found him in his cabin.

There were three ships on the mission to explore and chart the waters around the eastern side of Antarctica. One was a destroyer, one a sea plane tender and one a tanker carrying fuel for itself and the other two ships. The crew of the destroyer was not hand-picked for the mission. In fact, this was peacetime, immediately after World War II, and men were leaving the military, not joining. To make up the full compliment of 350 men, the Navy allowed naval prisoners to volunteer to serve as crew in lieu of completing their sentences. Some 60 of these ex-prisoners were part of the crew.

In 1946 technology was not what it is today. Charts of the waters around Antarctica did not exist. The ship had to rely on its own instruments to measure the depth of the waters. The skies were usually overcast so it was not uncommon to go for days without a true navigational fix on the location of the ship. In fact when one of the ships radioed to set up a rendezvous, it sometimes took three or four days to find each other.

Three ships, all part of the same exercise, in uncharted waters, with an inexperienced Captain on the destroyer with an inexperienced group of officers and an inexperienced crew at 65° S latitude.

One day a sea plane left the tender with a crew of five on board to fly out over the ice covered land. There was a crash and the pilot was badly burned though the rest of the crew received only minor injuries. Because of the location of the crash site, and the fact that there was no icebreaker among the three ships, the rescue plan unfolded moment by moment. The pilot was dragged across the ice by his fellow crew members to an area of open water where the sea plane could land and pick them up. Three of the survivors were eventually transferred to the destroyer. The pilot had suffered severe frost bite and gangrene was taking its toll on his feet and hands.

After many days, the ships made contact with an aircraft carrier on maneuvers westward of Little

America and transferred the pilot in a basket suspended on a line running between the destroyer and the carrier. As Dick describes it, standing on deck of the destroyer watching the transfer was like looking up at a seven story building. The weather was rough and the destroyer was taking water over the bow, however, on the larger, more stable carrier the men were playing basketball on the hanger deck.

As Dick relates the experience years afterwards, he still recalls that this was an unnerving responsibility for a young man. Though he had been trained well, being at the command of a ship in waters for which the seas were not charted meant that the depth of the water was made known at the very moment the ship was plying through the broken ice floes. It seemed that one minute you could have 1500 fathoms below and the next it was only 15 fathoms. Visibility was limited. Experience was lacking. Responsibility for 350 men could weigh heavily on one's mind. Accompanying these thoughts and reminders, however, is a strong sense of accomplishment and self-confidence.

Guiding a ship through uncharted waters in the Antarctica is not that different from guiding an individual life through an environment of change or a large corporation through the changing market place. The level of experience may not be the best, those surrounding you may not be of your choosing, the way may not be clearly charted, and you may be as mis-matched in your environment as a destroyer is to an aircraft carrier. Your only choice is to go forward.

At times it may appear that by cautiously moving along you will be safe. But just as Dick discovered the quick changes in the depth of the water beneath the ship, you may discover that the bottom is not as far away from you as you thought. Suddenly it comes up to meet you just when you had thought it was safe to remain on course.

We'd wager that Dick didn't have a true understanding when he set out for the Antarctica of what he would be facing. He did, however, display the attributes of a master during the experience. He had: (1) taken full advantage of the training that was available from the U. S. Navy; (2) brought his own unique life experiences and abilities to the event; (3) learned all he could about the unfamiliar environment in which he found himself so he could take necessary risks; and (4) was willing to remain flexible and creative.

Too often we choose to view our personal or organizational environment as a surfer venturing out into the waves created by a machine in a theme park. Each wave is nearly perfect, predictable in timing and intensity, and a great place to learn to surf or swim in the ocean. You are surrounded by life guards in the event something goes wrong and you can take a break when you begin to tire. Over a period of time as you take part in this activity your skills are improved and challenging the surf becomes easier. The only thing wrong with this picture is that you never leave the theme park and you never learn how to handle the unexpected.

On the other hand, watch the surfers as they ride the crashing waves off the shores of Hawaii. They are ever watchful for just the right wave, one that will give them a longer, more exciting ride. They are not afraid to let some waves pass them by. Instead they are disciplined in selecting the right wave for them.

After the wave has been selected the surfer makes sure he is positioned at the right spot on the wave, staying on the crest. If he falls behind, he doesn't get the full potential the wave can offer. If he gets impatient and gets ahead of the crest he is overwhelmed by the wave, pulled under and tossed about.

Notice that for the surfer in the real ocean there are no two waves the same, no two rides the same, no two days the same. You can also tell the seasoned surfers from the novices. Those beginning to learn the sport first come to watch others to observe techniques. At first they mimic the pros but in time develop their own unique style. As they become more experienced they improve their ability to make judgements about the waves, taking less time and making more correct decisions. They continue to learn more about their sport whether it is the changing technology applied to their equipment or the nuances of the natural elements that surround them. Flexibility and creativity soon follow as they challenge themselves, the elements and their fellow competitors.

Unfortunately, the real world is not made up of theme park wave machines. Too bad, because then our old ways of approaching the issues in life by coping and managing would be adequate. In the realm of change which is reality today, success belongs to the one who has attained mastery.

The Change Master who chooses to apply the four principles of mastery will be amazed at how much enjoyment will be found in the journey.

fa-mil-iar (fə-mil´yər) *adj.* Often encountered; common; having knowledge of something

CHAPTER FOUR

LOOKING BEYOND THE FAMILIAR

It was a dark and stormy night.....which explains why flights were being cancelled or delayed at the Tulsa airport. In fact my flight was now three hours late and the third delay announcement had just been made. What do you do at the Tulsa airport after the snack bars are closed and you can't even get a cup of coffee?

The only activity in the terminal was taking place around one of the scanning machines at the entry point to the gates. Curious, I joined the group of four individuals clustered around the machine. I soon discovered this was a training class where operators were being taught to detect prohibited items among the bags passing before them. Standing on the periphery of the group watching the process for some time, I soon became proficient at identifying lipstick, combs, pens, alarm clocks, etc. Noticing my curiosity, I was invited to step up to the machine and take the test. Unfortunately, two guns and a knife went by undetected. There were so many familiar and interesting shapes, so much to observe, and it was all happening so fast. How, I asked, did anyone ever learn to identify all the objects.

The trainer then explained that like others at the beginning of the process, I was focusing on trying to identify the familiar. The secret was to screen out everything in the background and look only for the items that were to be detected. Given this piece of advice, we started the process again, and my ability to recognize the offensive items improved dramatically.

This experience clearly defines the issues surrounding mastering change in our lives. To become a Change Master, one must be able to screen out the familiar.

R. Buckminster Fuller, a Nobel Peace Prize recipient, best known as the inventor of the geodesic dome, writing in 1969 in *Operating Manual for Spaceship Earth,* postulated that it was possible to predict trends for the next twenty-five years. He states:

> *I recall that in 1927 I set about deliberately exploring to see how far ahead we could make competent forecasts regarding the direction in which all humanity is trending*

and to see how effectively we could interpret the physical details of what comprehensive evolution might be portending as disclosed by the available data. I came to the conclusion that it is possible to make a fairly reasonable forecast of about twenty-five years. That seems to be about one industrial "tooling" generation. On the average, all inventions seem to get melted up about every twenty-five years, after which the metals come back into recirculation in new and usually more effective uses."

Fuller went on to predict several uses of computers and systems thinking, all of which were borne out in the intervening years.

Faith Popcorn, writing in *The Popcorn Report* in 1991 states that *no one knows (exactly) how the future will feel and unfold, but the trends are pushing us there with a force that's almost tangible.* Extricating trends from the familiar is the basis for Popcorn's consultation practice in assisting clients in understanding the needs of tomorrow's customers.

Why then is it so difficult for most of us to see these trends and take advantage of the knowledge to make appropriate changes in our personal lives or business practices? The answer to that question is that we are most comfortable when surrounded by the familiar. Familiarity brings with it a certain aura of calm accompanied by memories of times past which can be extrapolated to expectations of what will happen tomorrow.

Isn't familiarity what tradition is all about? Doesn't familiarity give a better perspective on problem solving? While there are instances when the answer to these questions is "yes," the truth is that in demanding that we see only the familiar, we force ourselves to become locked into a status quo mode which is woefully inadequate for living in an environment where change is the norm.

There is less stress and more enjoyment for those individuals who adapt the skill of screening out the familiar. Looking beyond the familiar is an effective way to prepare for tomorrow, whether that tomorrow is 24 hours or 24 years in the future. The skill is developed by applying two principles: (1) accept the speed at which change is occurring, and (2) venture out of your area of expertise to locate the trends.

The first principle is to accept the fact that the speed at which change occurs is dramatically increasing. There is no lack of evidence to support this statement.

Take a look at the time it takes for products to become commercially successful. The fluorescent bulb, for example, was invented and tested eighty-two years before it was successfully brought to market. On the other hand, the transistor took only ten years from inception to market. In the ten years between 1983 and 1993, the number of personal computers in United States offices increased by 25,000,000.

Perhaps evidence that the speed of change has had an effect on our personal lives can be seen in the fact that annual sales of over-the-counter pain relievers increased by $500,000,000 in the six years between 1987 and 1993!

In the University of Illinois Showcase of Tomorrow in 1958, one of the most popular demonstrations was the microwave which was touted as representing the "future" of cooking. That muffins could be cooked in just a few minutes and come out of the oven in dishes that were cool to the touch was a "miracle" and certainly not considered a feasible addition to America's kitchens in the foreseeable future. Less than fifteen years later microwave ovens began appearing in the marketplace and today are found in nearly every home and college dorm room in America.

Another example of the speed at which change is

occurring is the time it takes for major scientific discoveries to move from theory to practical application. It was seventy years before the scientific breakthroughs of Isaac Newton were technologically applied to create the machines that ultimately launched the industrial revolution. It took fifty years for Albert Einstein's discoveries to usher in the nuclear age. The field of genetic engineering was spawned in slightly less than thirty-five years after the 1953 discovery by Watson and Crick of the helical structure of the genetic substance DNA. We can only speculate on the impact of the theory of imaginary time contained in a manuscript on understanding the universe submitted in 1984 by Stephen Hawking. The book, *A Brief History of Time*, was on the bestseller lists for more than 100 weeks and has showcased Hawking's desire to open new ways of understanding the very nature of our universe.

Those who refuse to accept and adapt to the speed of change find themselves not only frustrated but unable to regain ground lost by refusing to identify and incorporate change into their personal lives or their businesses.

The second principle for success is to put aside the familiar and actively look for the unfamiliar to identify early trends leading to the next wave of change. The way to begin is by looking outside your area of expertise or industry, observe what is happening and creatively apply what you learn to your own situation.

Who would have thought that automobiles would be made affordable for the masses because of the practices of the meat packinghouses of Chicago in the early 1900's? Henry Ford was one of what had to be hundreds of outsiders to tour a packinghouse. The revolution in the meat industry was the invention in the late 1800's of an overhead chain system that allowed a carcass to be moved from place to place within the facility. Up until that time the carcass remained stationary and butchering occurred in one place, a slow and inefficient process. Gus Schmidt of the Cincinnati Butcher Supply Company in 1906 patented the first jerkless chain system for the slaughter industry. Previous attempts to move carcasses by chain had failed because a line that jerked would cause the carcass to fall, sometimes injuring the workers in the process. With the advent of the jerkless chain, animal carcasses could be moved smoothly through the facility with people stationed safely along the way to dismantle the carcass into cuts of meats for retailers and consumers. While others went through a packinghouse and observed how a carcass was turned into the familiar cuts of meat seen at the corner butcher shop, Ford observed the process. He saw an operation designed to disassemble a whole product into parts. By reversing the process, he theorized, one could take individual parts and turn them into a whole product. Thus the assembly line for economically and efficiently producing automobiles was conceived.

Luigi Galvani was trained in medicine, not in electricity. His research on how muscles and nerves conduct electricity became the basis of his invention of the electric battery. Fred Smith's original business idea for Federal Express was to fly Federal Reserve cash from region to region to save the government approximately $3 million a day in financial float. The contract with the government never materialized so Smith ended up in the aviation repair business in Arkansas. His frustration with the time it took to receive parts for his business led to the launching of Federal Express to deliver overnight packages.

History is full of similar examples of individuals who have stepped outside the familiarity of their own expertise. By allowing the limitations of the familiar backdrop to fade away, much like focusing on the clutter passing through the airport scanning machine cleverly disguised the objects of potential danger, these individuals developed processes and products that were revolutionary.

To obtain the skills required to fade the background, it is necessary to understand how the human brain "sees" an object or event.

Behavioral scientists have known for many years that we really don't *see* what we're seeing. It is more correct to say we are interpreting and making judgments based on our individual past experience or education about what we are observing, which in turn becomes our reality.

The science of optics began in ancient times with the first learned writing attributed to the philosopher and mathematician, Euclid, in about 300 BC, who introduced perspective into geometrical theory. However, the controversy between vision as an active process of a living human eye rather than the passive recording of physical impressions from the outside continued throughout the Middle Ages. The active eye theory stated that the eye itself was not an optical instrument and that mankind saw only with the soul. After all, it was argued, how could large images, like those of mountains, possibly squeeze through the tiny pupil of the eye. It was not until Kepler in the early 17th century that the first reasonably complete description of the way that the lens of the eye forms an image on the retina was documented.

However, behavioral scientists, digesting research gathered on individuals recovering from strokes and those whose sight had been restored, began adding new information on sight in the 1950's. The subjects of those studies were describing objects that were fragmented and not connected. They would see "parts" of an object before them, but were not always able to comprehend the parts as a connected whole. For example, some described looking at a loved one and seeing an arm that appeared to be "floating" next to the body. Using pictures and other means of recognition, these subjects were eventually taught to recognize the "parts" as a whole unit.

Therein lies the distinction in understanding how we observe things. We now know that the brain accepts only 20% of the actual physical attributes of the object being projected onto the retina to define what it sees. The remaining 80% of that picture is garnered from information already contained in the memory. Observing a small child learning to recognize familiar objects is one way to illustrate this phenomenon. At one point, anything that is furry, has four legs and moves is a "doggie." Only with patient teaching and subsequent experience does the child learn the difference between dogs, cows, kittens and other four-legged animals. Thereafter every four-legged animal that comes into their sight is recognized for specific attributes (20%) and then determined from memory and/or experience (80%) to be a specific species which then makes up the total picture.

The following illustration will assist in understanding what occurs. The brain receives information in the form of a series of dots or pixels which are seen as:

●or ○

It then takes this random information and seeks to enhance that which is familiar thereby bringing an image into your conscious mind. Once that familiar image is accepted and registered, you are ready to move on to something else, satisfied that you have gathered the meaning of what you are seeing.

To show you how this works, take a look at the illustration on the next page.

When you first looked at the picture you probably saw the patterns of light and shadow on the page. By blocking out this image, you may begin to "see" a dog emerge from the page. However, if you look more closely, you will realize there is no outline of the animal. The fact is that both possibilities exit within the same illustration. The one that exists for you depends on the 80% of your memory or experience that was chosen to be applied while seeking the familiar.

Illustration above is used by permission from *The Enchanted Loom* by Robert Jastrow ©1981 by Reader's Library, Inc.

The propensity to seek order and familiarity also finds itself in our physical activities and actions.

Mark Twain, writing in *The Adventures of Huckleberry Finn*, describes a raft trip down the Mississippi River shared by Huck and a runaway slave named Jim. A man was dead and Jim had been falsely targeted as the leading suspect. Huck and his friend took to the Mississippi to make their escape. After days of drifting down the river they made plans for Huck to go ashore to find out exactly where they were. Having acquired a trunk of clothing along the way, it was decided that Huck would go disguised as a girl so he would not be recognized and expose Jim's whereabouts. Huck spent an entire day learning how to act like a girl before setting off in a canoe for shore. Once on land, Huck eventually found himself at a house where the mistress was home. She invited him in for a visit and some food and all went well until Huck began to thread a needle. This caused the mistress to suspect that perhaps the young "lady" in her midst was in reality a young "man." To find out if she was right, she tossed a lump of lead into Huck's lap while his hands were busy holding a hank of yarn she had been winding into a ball. Instantly, he clapped his legs together to catch the object thrown at him rather than make a basket out of his skirt by throwing his knees apart. It was the threading of the needle that first raised the mistress' suspicions. As she later pointed out to Huck, men bring the needle to the thread; women hold the needle steady and bring the thread to its eye. Her suspicions were confirmed by the way Huck "caught" the lump of lead.

We react as instinctively when responding to the world around us based on familiarity. No matter how hard we try to convince ourselves that we have become objective, without a conscious effort to explore the patterns and models through which we filter our world, we are doomed to ultimately respond by the old rules.

Ironically, we can return to the history of optics to recognize that the active eye theory with its belief that mankind saw only with the soul was not totally wrong for it is the combination of observing with the soul and the mechanics of the working of the lens that leads to understanding and creativity.

Architect Frank Lloyd Wright exploited the secret of incorporating soul into the mechanics of architecture. One of his most famous structures, Fallingwater, is a prime example. Edgar Kaufman, Jr. commissioned Wright to build a weekend cottage on property in Pennsylvania where a beautiful waterfall and ravine known as Bear Run was located. Kaufman asked

Wright to place the cottage on the side of the ravine that would allow him to take full advantage of the view of the waterfall, preferably slightly above the fall itself. When Wright visited the site, he immediately saw more than the waterfall and ravine. Meryle Secrest, writing in *Frank Lloyd Wright, A Biography,* describes the moment Fallingwater began to crystalize in Wright's mind:

> *As he (Wright) worked, he kept up a running commentary: 'The rock on which E. J. (Kaufman) sits will be the hearth, coming right out of the floor, the fire burning just behind it. The warming kettle will fit into the wall here...Steam will permeate the atmosphere. You'll hear the hiss...'*

The cantilevered house, which in itself was a break from traditional architectural design, would be located over the falls so that those who resided within would become a part of the experience of running water, solid rock and the winds of nature. Everyone who has visited or lived in the house excitedly describes the feelings the house located over the falls brings forth. The emotions that are a result of the experience are described as being far more powerful and memorable than merely looking at the falls would have ever been. All this because Wright looked at the waterfall and saw more than just water rushing down the side of the ravine.

Just as a mechanical view of a mountain reveals only a pile of rocks and dirt covered with vegetation, the soul of the photographer will see an object of beauty made up also of flora, streams, living creatures and patterns of shadow and light. Soul, apart from the familiar definition of spirituality or the eternal essence of an individual, is more broadly defined as that which is the central or vital part of something. In other words, by seeking to find the soul of a trend or process or event, we are seeking the meaning behind what we are seeing or experiencing. Once we have come to an understanding of the meaning or purpose, then the familiar begins to quickly drop away and new possibilities abound.

In reviewing an except from Edwin Schrodinger's 1959 book, *Science and Humanism: Physics in Our Time*, John Newman, in 1956, writes:

> *The excerpt deals in lively and lucid fashion with a variety of the profound changes which experimental and mathematical physics have brought about in our picture of the physical world. Schrodinger discusses the nature of our physical models, the concepts of*

continuity and causality -- or rather what is now left of the older, comfortable versions of these ideas -- and the mathematical discipline known as wave-mechanics, of which he is the founder. It is a brilliant performance; when you have gone through it your picture of the world will, I promise, be both clearer and more topsy-turvy than ever before.

This is a description of what happens when the familiar background is screened out. The world becomes both clearer and more topsy-turvy than ever before.

In retrospect, the world around us takes on clarity only when we put aside the familiar. The first key is to accept that change is occurring around us at ever increasing speed. The sunrise we saw this morning will not be the same as the one we view tomorrow, yet each event is described as a sunrise. We must search diligently in the familiar events around us to observe the subtle and not so subtle changes that are constantly taking place. Look beyond the front page of the newspaper to the small items tucked in the back or in filler spaces. There you will see snippets of information often describing an event or discovery that will one day explode into the mainstream. Or, over a period of time, you will discover a common thread or idea among those small insignificant articles that will propel you into seeing beyond the familiar.

To apply the second key principle of stepping out of your own area of expertise, the secret is learning to see with your soul, to search for the meaning or purpose that lies within the event. One way to acquire this skill is to look around you to identify those individuals who always seem to be on the cutting edge. You will find they are all normal human beings just like you, but they have developed the uncanny ability to become a part of the experience of life itself by applying all their senses to everything they do. Henry Ford applied logic and knowledge of assembling automobiles to the process of slaughtering an animal in the packinghouses. Huck gave himself away because he didn't recognize the need to change a habit. We, like Huck, often fall back to doing the familiar in a new situation because we do not accept the challenge of changing a habit. Society delights in those individuals or businesses that have overcome obstacles to achieve success. We are all driven to succeed. These pioneers share a common trait; they each made a conscious effort to seek the soul or meaning behind what was happening around them, were willing to step outside the familiar, and then creatively apply their new understanding to attain success. In short, they chose, willingly or unwillingly, to put aside the familiar and respond to life in a new way. Just as easily we can look at individuals and businesses that have fallen by the wayside in history because they refused to venture beyond the familiar and, against all odds, would not relinquish the status quo. They too made a choice.

Responding in totally new ways to what happens in your world requires experimentation, exploration and enthusiastic embracing of the unfamiliar and uncomfortable. It is not easy at first and sometimes the solutions we derive from the exercise may seem impossible. But we should not shy away from impossibilities for therein lies the experience of seeing things anew.

A conversation between Alice and the Queen in Louis Caroll's *Through the Looking Glass* describes our reluctance to actively seek the unfamiliar:

> *"'I can't believe that,' said Alice.*
>
> *'Can't you?' the Queen said in pitying tone. "Try again: draw a long breath and shut your eyes.'*
>
> *Alice laughed: 'There's no use in trying,' she said; 'one can't believe impossible things.'*

'I daresay you haven't had much practice,' said the Queen. 'When I was younger, I always did it for half an hour a day. Why, sometimes I've believed as many as six impossible things before breakfast.'"

Like Alice, we refuse to believe in "impossible" things. Yet the "impossible" often becomes reality. At one time it was impossible to instantly transmit exact copies of documents to another place; today Facsimile (FAX) machines make it a routine activity. At one time it was impossible to think of having a powerful computer that would fit on a desktop; today one can fit in your briefcase. You can probably think of your own "impossible" things to add to the list. These "impossibles," even when positive, create stress. Expectations and routines are disrupted and valuable energy is expended in absorbing the new. Stress can be mitigated, however, when change is anticipated. What better reason for continuing to refine the skills necessary to detect future trends, and see beyond the familiar backdrop.

It was a dark and stormy night and the Change Master learned an important lesson. Screening out the familiar background is the beginning of the exciting journey toward mastering change. Seeking different patterns and pictures, responding in new ways, and honing skills is the difference between becoming an agent of change or a casualty of change.

Purpose (porpoise) *n* result or effect that is intended or desired; intention

Vision (vizh'en) n 2. unusual foresight

CHAPTER FIVE

YESTERDAY, TODAY AND TOMORROW

Business and personal help sections of bookstores are lined with books extolling the need to develop a mission or vision statement. We are told that those with a vision for the future are destined to become all they dream or desire to become. Yet there are far more organizations and individuals with visions than there are those who succeed in achieving their dreams. What is the difference? Lengthy research into the lives of individuals and histories of organizations coupled with research on quantum physics and the new science has led us to the discovery of the answer to that question. The key lies in understanding the relationship between purpose and vision. Purpose without vision has no future; vision without purpose has no meaning.

Total Quality Management (by whatever name), empowered teams, re-engineering, self-organizing systems and participative management are goals many organizations have sought to achieve. According to *Harvard Business Review, Industry Week* and *Fortune*, the actual results have been lackluster. So much promise, so little success. Sometimes the lack of success is attributable to lack of total commitment, but more often it can be traced to lack of not understanding purpose. This applies to individuals as well as organizations.

Vision statements are usually developed in a vacuum, focused entirely on the future without regard to the past. The usual practice is to engage in exercises that lead to envisioning the future of the organization. That future is then distilled into a vision statement to be shared with other managers, and perhaps with the entire workforce. For a vision to be relevant and attainable, the past cannot be ignored. Stated as an equation, the key is as follows:

Purpose + Actions + Vision = Success

Purpose is the past. Actions are the present activities of the individual or organization. Vision is the future.

Picture yourself or your organization as a ship. If you were asked the most important role on that vessel, the answer would most likely be the Captain. It is the Captain, after all, that sets the course, directs the crew, and arrives at the desired destination. Overlooked is the fact that the Captain climbs aboard a ship that already exists. In reality, the most important role is the ship's designer. The designer has created the past, the purpose, for the vessel. An oil tanker is not a pleasure ship. Suppose the Captain aboard the oil tanker has developed a vision of being the best luxury cruise liner in the Caribbean. Assume the level of commitment, persistence and resources are of the highest quality. Unless the past of that vessel is understood and acknowledged, the Captain will sacrifice himself and the crew pursuing a dream for which they were ill-equipped.

A review of organizations that have attempted to implement TQM gives a rich example of how this works. Motorola, Xerox, Florida Power & Light and many other businesses, large and small, are examples of the tremendous success to be gained from TQM. Other Fortune 500 companies have also expended resources to achieve the same results, but have fallen far short of their expectations.

A close examination reveals that there are two factors involved in individuals and businesses who are successful. The first is they possess a strong sense of urgency. The second is they have grasped a thorough understanding of their past.

Urgency is too often confused with crisis. A crisis is an unexpected turn of events that requires immediate attention for survival. Urgency involves something that is of immediate import or significance.

Remember the story you heard as a child about the ant and the grasshopper? It was one of Aesop's tales, and like all fables attributed to this 6th century writer, it contains a moral. In this story a grasshopper confronts an ant who is diligently putting away the fruits of the harvest. The grasshopper, busy playing his fiddle and taking life easy, takes delight in ridiculing the ant for putting away food in the midst of beautiful weather and a bountiful harvest where there appears to be plenty. However, as winter settles on the land, the scene changes and the grasshopper is now found frantically beating on the door to the ant's home begging to be let in out of the cold and allowed to share the food the ant has put away.

When things were going well and resources were plentiful, the grasshopper saw no need to do other than enjoy the respite. The ant recognized the principle that even when it doesn't appear to be urgent to complete an assignment, begin a project or take the competition seriously, it is important to maintain a sense of urgency and prepare for the future. He was keenly aware that summer and fall would not last forever and that in harsher times he would need to have additional reserves and provisions.

That principle of consistently preparing for change and the future is what has set apart successful individuals and businesses from the rest of the pack. They have recognized that the environment in which they find themselves today will not be the same tomorrow. As a result by creating a sense of urgency in preparing for tomorrow, they become more creative and flexible and take advantage of the energy created by positive stress.

The second factor that is shared by successful individuals and businesses is that they openly and honestly explored their past. In doing so they discovered what they did well, what they needed to improve, what business they thought they were in, what business practices they actually embraced, how they viewed their industry, how people within the organization interfaced with one another, what values and beliefs were prevalent among the workforce, etc. By undertaking this exercise, the purpose of the organization is made known. Armed with this insight, visions that stretched the organization to new heights while acknowledging its past were developed. As a result, the crew could accept sprucing up an oil tanker to take on new opportunities.

The organization that has dropped TQM into its culture without understanding its past has created a vision with no purpose for those within the organization. At first it was exciting to try something new, but the old culture, the past history, was not impacted and soon it was business as usual. Management threw up their hands and the program was abandoned amid shaking heads and the rush to find the next hot idea. In the aftermath valuable individuals and processes were disrupted or destroyed and morale was eroded.

This happens to individuals as well as organizations. Change your habits. Try something new. Dream big dreams. This is the advice found in all the leading self-help books and articles. All offer only band-aid approaches to a vision for the future unless time is taken to understand the past. Every life has a purpose; every life has a past. In that past lies beliefs, values and experiences that together define the purpose.

Understanding and incorporating purpose into developing a vision does not mean that the future is limited. Once the purpose is known, then any necessary changes to the purpose can be wrought. That oil tanker will need major renovation to become a luxury liner, but it is not impossible. However, some of its past purpose will not be lost in the process. For example, the hull will still be designed for plodding through the waters carrying oil, not passengers. The action plans developed for reaching the vision of being a luxury liner will take that fact into account.

What happens when the purpose of the organization is ignored in the development of a vision? Let's look at a couple of examples.

A business with which we have consulted was part of a merger. The purpose of the two organizations were very different. One culture was old-line and came from a long and illustrious past. The purpose of that business was to be a low-cost producer. The other culture was newer and based on a sense of family with very few rules and many social gatherings to celebrate small successes. The purpose of that business was to be innovative and energetic. The companies were brought together with a new and exciting vision, one that was very appropriate for its resources and competencies. However, the past of these companies were not factored into the formula and never addressed. People were left confused and the two businesses have remained, in effect, separate, neither group understanding the other. Synergies that were seen as assets at the time of the merger have not been realized and after five years, there is little progress toward reaching the vision. Every achievement has been gained by dragging the organization along with the crews, kicking and screaming all the way.

Another organization with which we have consulted was a take-over. The culture was one of hostility between management and labor and incorporated processes that had been in place for all the years the plant had been in operation. The new owner envisioned empowered teams, gainsharing, pay-for-skills and a work environment that was fun. Recognizing that the past defined the purpose, this new owner took precious time to meet with individuals from the rank and file, as well as management, to explore what was good about the past, what could be changed, whether it was important to make changes, and what the organization could become. By incorporating the past, major changes were accomplished without destroying the underlying purpose. Within a year the plant had developed empowered work teams, gainsharing and a respect for all individuals at all levels -- and it was a fun, and profitable, place to work!

Change will ultimately destroy the vision of the

individual or organization that has ignored its purpose. The Change Master will take the time to explore and acknowledge purpose before developing a vision.

Those who master change recognize that purpose without vision has no future; vision without purpose has no meaning.

awareness (ə-wâr′-ness) *n.* mindful or conscious of, cognizant

CHAPTER SIX

THE WART FACTOR

Welcome to the most informed civilization to have ever inhabited the earth. The age of information is here at last and with it the expectation that change will no longer be a threat because of the ability to access information on all subjects with little delay. The perception is that computers can plot the future, given enough information. Our obsession with staying informed is evidenced by the business card of today which is imprinted with a name, address, office phone number, mobile phone number, pager number, FAX number and Internet address. Information is indeed here -- but the effects of change are more rampant than ever. What went wrong?

The answer lies within a legend from the 12th Century. The legend usually begins at the moment when a small, scrawny child named Arthur confidently steps up to a stone in which the sword Excalibur was half buried. According to legend, the one who extracted Excalibur from the stone was to ascend to the throne. Many strong and capable men failed as they attempted to extract Excalibur in search of becoming King. As the legend unfolds, it is filled with adventure and wisdom culminating in accomplishments far ahead of their time. At the mere mention of the Knights of the Round Table, Queen Guinevere, Sir Lancelot or the mortal combat between Arthur and his nephew Mordred at the battle of Camlan can conjure up images from our reading, or from Lerner and Loewe's musical *Camelot.*

Overlooked too often are the lessons learned by Wart, the name Arthur was fondly given by Merlin, his tutor and mentor. Merlin, as you recall, was travelling backwards in time when he and Arthur first met in the woods. Theirs was a special and sometimes disturbing relationship. Merlin, having the advantage of knowing the future, was often unable to convey all that he had experienced to Arthur. Likewise, Arthur, having experienced the past was at a loss in explaining things to Merlin. However, within that relationship lies the key to Arthur's success. The secret Merlin imparted to Wart was to seek awareness before making any major decisions. That's it, pure and simple. Awareness. Awareness goes beyond information or understanding and is the foundation upon which a Change Master bases their success.

Arthur, as with most children, had a very high level of curiosity. Merlin wisely realized that by imparting the ability to be aware of all that was going on around him, Arthur would be best equipped to overcome the challenges of the future. When Arthur wanted to know about flying, swimming or hunting, Merlin would magically transform Wart into a bird, a fish or an animal of prey through Arthur's imagination. By pretending he was one of these animals Arthur was made keenly aware of the limitations and possibilities of each imaginary metamorphis. He could, for example, understand why a fish might never be aware of the water surrounding it until taken out of the water. These exercises gave Wart an insightful sensitivity for values, character and the ability to seek unique methods of survival in unfamiliar environments. Wart had learned to go beyond information and understanding.

Information and understanding, while valuable assets, do not provide the depth of flexibility and creativity necessary to master change. To better comprehend this distinction between information, understanding and awareness, let's examine each attribute in more detail.

Information is not difficult to attain in today's world. We are surrounded by sources of information in simple and highly sophisticated formats. In the remote areas of Africa people huddle around television sets to watch programs coming from all corners of the world made available via satellites.

The latest information glut comes into our homes and offices via the information highway, known as Internet. In 1973 Dr. Vinton Cerf was attending a conference on computers in San Francisco when he sketched much of the structure of the Internet computer network on the back of an envelope. He is known among cyberspace fans as the "Father of the Internet." His principal contribution was the development of the TCP/IP computer language which enabled computers within several networks located all over the world to be connected to a common network. Thus, Internet was born. It only took two decades to become a reality. The next step, according to Dr. Cerf, is to incorporate intelligent agents -- software programs that can seek out only the materials from the morass of information on the Internet that would be of interest to the user. We will not be without information as we speed into the 21st Century! We will experience a new source of stress. In the past we were stressed because of lack of information with which to make decisions; today we are stressed because of the sheer quantity and diversity of information.

If Dr. Cerf is successful in implementing intelligent software to seek out information of interest, it still is nothing more than raw data, sometimes organized and sometimes in random format. Information by itself is useless. It is only when there is relevance that information takes on meaning. For example, the information in a 1989 New York University report indicated that "of all scientists who ever lived, 85% are alive today." Interesting and informative, but not necessarily useful, unless you are working with an issue relating to science or scientists.

Any specific piece of information is available to many individuals or organizations at the same time. Why then aren't there more Dr. Cerfs? More Galileos? More Einsteins? Because information is not the key to mastering change.

There is another factor concerning information which substantiates that it alone is not the key to mastering change. Information can be as misleading as it can be valuable. One of the first things that comes to mind are all the studies on any given health issue. It seems that as soon as one study is published and the information diligently disseminated to the public, another comes along and refutes the data. A recent motion picture, *Forrest Gump,* filmed in 1994, shows the main character interacting with individuals who are no longer living. Virtual reality is not much more than a novelty as this book is being written. Individuals pay a fee to experience a world that does not exist. Those who are spectators watch the main subject physically react to what is going on in imaginary time and space.

If information is not the key, perhaps understanding is the missing piece. Understanding goes beyond being informed and is defined as "comprehending the meaning or significance of something." Understanding is built on knowledge gained from a combination of information and experience. Symbolically, we refer to "a light going on" in our heads when we reach that point of understanding how something works. While it is easy to obtain information, progressing to the level of understanding requires greater commitment and effort.

Many years of formal education are often required to attain the knowledge necessary to truly understand a subject. Another way of gaining understanding is from a hobby or under the tutelage of a mentor.

The difference between one who appears successful and finds enjoyment in his or her avocation and life in general, and one who is not, is that the successful individual or organization has committed the resources necessary to gain the depth of knowledge and experience to understand their area of interest. Some are committed enough to become experts and are recognized as such by others. Organizations can also become experts in their core competencies. Wal☆Mart has redefined the distribution system for retailers; L. L. Bean has defined customer service; and Federal Express is widely known for its ability to move packages overnight despite obstacles. Reaching a level of understanding places an individual or organization in a more competitive posture.

In the past, survival and success came to the business that acquired the necessary information and understanding of the industry in which it was engaged or, in the case of individuals, the one who acquired information and understanding of the nuances of a particular subject matter. The paradox is that often experts become so engrossed in their expertise that awareness is never reached. The real breakthroughs and overwhelming successes belong to those who have gone beyond information and understanding to reach awareness.

A closer look at the evolution of benchmark organizations will uncover the fact that while they remained committed to their core competency they were willing to make necessary adjustments to insure that they stayed at the top of their industry. These organizations maintained their focus on trends. In the 1950's a product needed to be low-cost to compete for the consumer's dollar. Competition soon shifted to providing quality to the consumer. While cost was still important, it was not the only basis of the decision to buy. The economy changed and by the 1960's as technology improved, consumers began to base their decision to buy on the quality and reliability of the product, and were willing to pay more for these attributes. Lifestyles changed again in the 1980's with the majority of families made up of dual wage-earners. Time became a precious commodity and service was an added factor in making choices. Keep in mind that lower cost and quality did not go away. Those attributes were now a given in the minds of the consumer. The consumer demanded that service be added to the formula. In the 1990's it is style that sets products apart. The style in which the service is provided, or product is presented is most important.

An example of this shift can be seen in the evolution of the television set. As television burst upon the airways in the late 1940's, early sets were very functional though not always reliable. As consumers flocked to the stores to buy television sets, there was little to distinguish one from the other. The decision to buy was based upon price first, reputation of the company second. The Japanese soon realized that low cost was a key factor and entered the television market with a vengeance. But they added a new twist, low cost *plus* quality.

The quality factor was introduced because the Japanese looked at a problem they were facing in a new way and became aware that they could not compete on the basis of maintenance. Television sets were being sold in as diverse locations as drug stores. When a television set needed maintenance, it was very expensive for the Japanese to service their sets. U.S. television manufacturers had established locations for handling necessary repairs. To solve the problem, the Japanese decided to add a level of quality to their products, making them more reliable, and thus less apt to need repair. It became more cost effective to replace the customer's set rather than establish locations for making repairs. Consumers quickly realized that there was a difference between the television sets now appearing in the marketplace and quality became as important as price, though quality at a reasonable price was still a driving factor. Televisions today are trouble-free, user friendly, versatile (to take advantage of interactive opportunities), and price competitive. What the consumer wanted next was service.

A personal example of service occurred when a Sony

television with a one year warranty on parts and which had been owned for about four years began to malfunction. After only two brief calls to the company requesting assistance in finding appropriate locations for repairing the set, a representative was on the phone to authorize a complete replacement, no questions asked. Sony arranged for the delivery of the new set, which was the latest model and therefore better than the set owned, and picked up the old set at no cost.

The next issue is style. Style is defined as the way or manner in which something is done. Style goes beyond mere aesthetics of the design. Style is what sets one company apart from another, one individual apart from another. A recent visit to an electronics store led to the experience of new style. To decide on a television, you are ushered into a soundproof room, where the lighting can be adjusted to replicate your home environment, then you relax in a comfortable lounge chair with the remote in your hand to evaluate one of several sets available for sale. It was the next best thing to being at home.

We've established that information and understanding are important tools, but they are not the lone keys to becoming an agent of change. Awareness is what gives the Change Master an edge.

Let's return to Wart to understand the attributes of awareness whereby we gain unique insight. T. H. White, in describing the adventures of young Arthur and Merlin, has given us the formula for gaining this kind of awareness. Wart used his imagination to become a fish in order to gain understanding and knowledge of what it was like to be that fish. The paradox is that by "becoming" the object of his curiosity he gained the ability to stand outside that object, observe it from a new perspective, and, then by applying his experiences as a child to this new understanding of a fish, he achieved the creativity to overcome the unfamiliar.

In a universe of change we as individuals and organizations are daily coming face to face with unfamiliarity wrought by change. Accept the challenge of adopting the Wart Factor by being willing to use your imagination to "become" a process or object.

Dr. Jonas Salk of the Salk Institute for Biological Studies, best known for discovering the polio vaccine in 1955, has been a Wart all his life. In an early 1994 interview with editors of *Bottom Line/Personal*, Dr. Salk indicated that very early in life he would imagine what it would be like to be the object in which he was interested. To quote from the interview, Dr. Salk stated:

> *"After I became a scientist, I used this system to imagine myself as a virus or a cancer cell, for example, and to sense what it would be like.*
>
> *"I would also imagine myself as the immune system to reconstruct what I would do if engaged in combat with a virus or a cancer cell.*
>
> *"After I played through a series of scenarios on a particular problem and acquired new insight, I designed laboratory experiments accordingly.*
>
> *"Based on the results of these experiments, I would then know which questions to ask next -- until I learned what I wanted to know or until I went as far as I could go."*[1]

What Dr. Salk discovered was that by engaging in this activity of imagination and dialogue with himself he acquired a new perspective. As with Wart, when Salk was engaged in this activity, he became so engrossed in the imagination that he assumed the attributes of the object being studied. In this way he was not limited to the one perspective of the here and now, but was able to step outside and observe relationships and processes that were not evident before.

The Warts of the world quickly recognize that seeing from only one perspective is limiting. Getting outside of the here and now is necessary to explore the unfamiliar. You have more than likely reached this level of awareness from time to time, when you became immersed in the object of your concern. For example, have you ever had the experience of purchasing a new red car and suddenly the roadways are filled with red cars! They were there all along, but until you became Wart and experienced a red car from the perspective of an owner, you weren't aware of how many red cars were on the road.

Another example of gaining awareness is found once again in history. This time it is within the middle ages, during the time of the guilds. One began their journey into a profession by first becoming an apprentice. The focus during this phase of development, which could last for several years, was to work under a master to learn good work habits, speed and accuracy. The apprentice evolved from one who knew nothing about the trade to one who could efficiently replicate what had been taught. Upon attaining an acceptable level of ability, the apprentice was allowed to become a journeyman. During this phase of development individuals would focus on learning as many aspects of their craft as possible. A stonemason would use this time to work with other stonemasons and visit other cathedrals to see how they were made and to learn new approaches to what he had been taught. At a point in time the journeyman would be recognized as an artisan. There were basically two types of artisans. One had an in-depth knowledge of the various routines and subroutines required by his particular craft. The other had flexibility to shift from one routine to another so that he could meet specific customer desires. Paul Revere is an example of an artisan who had attained an in-depth knowledge of the craft of being a silversmith. Employing his own designs, he created bowls and pitchers following the exact steps each time, turning out marvelous pieces of silver. Another silversmith would use his knowledge to design specific pieces to meet the customer's wishes and then with his understanding of the craft would re-order the subroutines to create individual pieces that were not to be duplicated. An artisan had to be able to do many things well.

At the top of the hierarchy was the master. He too had acquired several skills and had attained artisan status. But by becoming immersed in his craft and in the world around him, he contributed three attributes beyond that of the artisan. The first skill was that of being inventive which led to the advancement of the craft. The second was the ability to teach others. And finally, he developed the methods of merchandising and attracting people to his wares. While remaining true to his competency, he had begun to experience the joy of the consumer, the artist and the craftsman and being aware of the nuances of each, had moved beyond focusing only on the craft.

By participating in the experience and acquiring the flexibility of new perspectives, any problem or process undergoing change, planned or unplanned, soon loses its unfamiliarity. Once information and understanding have been applied, one must step outside the situation and begin to assume the characteristics of the issue at hand. For example, in looking at a troubled process, begin to ask the questions: "If I were this process, what would be happening at this point, at that point, at the next point." "What would happen if I did this or that?" "What would make this step more efficient or less costly?" "Why do I have to do this step in this manner?" At first, this may seem awkward and will take more time and effort. Soon, however, it will become second nature.

Becoming like Wart works equally well for unplanned changes. Anyone can apply information and understanding to a situation. That is what has been done for years. It's the best way to maintain the status quo, but it does not meet the challenge for conditions brought about by change.

Try playing the role of Wart. With practice, you will be amazed at how easy and exciting it is to attain awareness. In the process you will have achieved the status of Change Master.

[1] *Bottom Line/Personal* published by Boardroom Reports June 15, 1994, volume 15, number 12 page 11.

paradigm (pâr′-ə-dīm) *n.* a pattern or model

CHAPTER SEVEN

BEYOND PARADIGM

Albert Einstein was once asked how he came to a totally new way of looking at physics than the way Isaac Newton and the rest of the scientific community looked at physics. Without hesitation he answered, "I questioned the axiom." In other words, he experienced a paradigm shift.

The concept of a paradigm shift is not new. Thomas Kuhn developed the concept in 1947 and described the role of paradigms in his 1962 book, *The Structure of Scientific Revolutions.* His premise was that when scientists went into an unknown area seeking understanding with a collective pattern or paradigm of expectation already in their minds of what they would find, then those findings that contradicted that expectation were discarded as unimportant or incorrect. In other words, the paradigm that pervaded at the outset was protected at all costs. He was the first to point out that the greatest advancements in the field of science occurred when individuals or groups who embraced a common belief concerning their area of expertise were so impacted by new evidence that they were willing to break away from the old and consider the new.

Joel Arthur Barker, the futurist, then turned paradigm into a recognized phenomenon when he pointed out in his 1985 book, *Discovering the Future, the business of paradigms,* that the majority of businesses which had failed were those who refused to change or question their paradigm. He convincingly argued that only when an organization recognizes their operating paradigm could they begin to see problems and opportunities for all they had to offer, thereby achieving greater success and stability.

Stephen Covey in his *Seven Habits of Highly Effective People* brought paradigm into our everyday vocabulary with his signature story of the man on the train with the children who were disturbing everyone. Only when it was learned that the man and his children had just left the deathbed of their wife and mother did the way the situation was viewed take a dramatic shift.

From irritation came compassion through understanding.

As Kuhn framed the concept of a paradigm shift, he envisioned a major shift in the thinking of not just one individual, but a group of individuals who had previously shared a common understanding. For example, a well-known shift in a society's paradigm of the world occurred because of the discoveries of Copernicus. Over four hundred years ago Copernicus proposed, in opposition to the prevailing theory that claimed the earth as the center of the universe with the heavens revolving around it, a theory in which the earth revolved on its axis and traveled around the sun with other heavenly bodies. Imagine the paradigm shift and its affect on science and society alike. From the beginning of recorded history it had been accepted without question that the earth was the center of the universe. However, after 1545, ordinary citizens as well as scientists were forced to accept that the very ground on which they stood was not only spinning on its axis, but was traveling through the heavens along with other planets, all circling around the sun.

To master change, it is necessary to fully understand the current paradigm from which a discipline, society or an individual operates. It is this pattern of the familiar, the experiences and memories, that must be questioned and perhaps put aside in order to detect the precursor of change that is occurring in our midst. A paradigm shift is not a momentary or passing variation in our pattern of viewing things. A true paradigm shift, as with Copernicus' theory, turns our world upside down. It is not comfortable. It does, however, lead to tremendous ability to absorb change and view the impact of future trends from a different perspective.

There is something more at work than just altering the way we view our world. Too often the paradigm shift is relegated to a specific incident or arena and once it has served its purpose, we return to our old way of thinking and doing things.

In addition, most of us are completely unaware of our paradigm and unable to separate ourselves from it. As a result, without our knowledge or our choice, it shapes what we are able to see and, therefore, what we allow ourselves to do and become. Perhaps Henri Matisse, the painter, put it best when he remarked: *there is nothing more difficult for a truly creative painter than to paint a rose, because before he can do so he has to first forget all the roses that were ever painted.*

To escape the bondage of our limited paradigm and

open ourselves and organizations to new possibilities, it is necessary in order to consciously make the effort to approach issues with a fresh perspective. Three attributes will be developed by the Change Master -- inspiration, aspiration and perspiration. These three attributes are necessary to understand the way we currently view our world. They are essential ingredients for breaking out of the ordinary.

The first attribute, inspiration, is defined as a "stimulation of the mind to a higher level." To put it another way, it is recognizing that by relegating ourselves or our business to becoming what others have determined we should be, we have settled for status quo. When our sense of who and what we are has been left to others to define, the effects of change will be not only disruptive but destructive.

To define who and what we are means we must discover what inspires us. To be inspired means finding the right star, the right niche, our unique gift or talent or product or service. This discovery process is one on which we must embark as an individual. Like the Wizard of Oz, inspiration is found within each individual and organization.

The most successful and proven way to begin this discovery process is to take time each morning, before turning to the news of the day, to define your own day and solicit your own focus. Sit down in a quiet place and with pen in hand begin to jot down ideas and thoughts in a personal journal. At first the writing may be rambling, may be shallow, may not come easily. But as you become more adept at giving yourself permission to take time out for this exercise, you will be astounded at the ideas, increased level of awareness and creativity that will result. In the process you will discover what is important to you and your organization and will find the source of your own inspiration.

History is full of individuals who were inspired to seek their own definition of self in spite of what others saw in them.

❐ The young man had been told repeatedly by his teacher that he had no voice and could not sing. He would be better off if he became the engineer his parents were encouraging him to become. The world would have lost the gift of a superb operatic voice if Enrico Caruso had listened to his teacher.

❐ Vince Lombardi was described as one who "possesses minimal football knowledge." And to top it off, he definitely lacked motivation.

❒ A violin student who preferred to play his own compositions instead of working on technique was told by his teacher that he was hopeless as a composer. Thankfully, Beethoven sought his own counsel.

❒ Albert Einstein didn't speak until he was four and couldn't read until he was seven. His teachers described him as "mentally slow, unsociable and adrift forever in his foolish dreams." He was expelled and was refused admittance to the Zurich Polytechnic School.

❒ Walt Disney was fired by a newspaper editor for lack of ideas and imagination.

These examples teach us that inspiration is very personal, very powerful and very necessary for true success.

Once you have gained an understanding of what inspires you, aspiration enters the picture. This is the desire that will motivate achievement. Desire is rooted in attitude and once again this is an attribute that comes from within and not from without.

Viktor E. Frankl, a renowned psychiatrist, developed a theory that man's primary motivational force is his search for meaning. This theory resulted from Dr. Frankl's experiences as a prisoner during years of unspeakable horror in Nazi death camps. Writing in 1959 in *Man's Search for Meaning,* Frankl offered this observation:

> *We who lived in the concentration camps can remember the men who walked through the huts comforting others, giving away their last piece of bread. They may have been few in number, but they offer sufficient proof that everything can be taken from a man but one thing: The last of his freedoms -- to choose one's attitude in any given set of circumstances, to choose one's own way.*

Aspiration, which is defined as a strong desire, has its roots in your attitude. No one defines your attitude but you. It is you alone who decides whether or not you will have a good day, week, month, year or lifetime. Your reaction to any given circumstance is all that matters.

On a visit to China, one of us had the opportunity to visit an American who was teaching English in one of the schools. She had been in China for several years and had subsisted on turnips, cabbage and fat pork. The accommodation was in a crowded house with dirt floors. There were no modern conveniences and the home was not even heated. Yet the individual was extremely happy and was convinced her work was worthwhile and rewarding. Her attitude was reflected in her own life and obviously had a positive effect on those around her.

Conditions and circumstances are neither good nor bad in and of themselves. The attitude of the individual or organization in perceiving, accepting and challenging the circumstances defines their ultimate power.

The freedom to choose your own way is too often taken for granted and too easily forfeited by the lack of not making any choice. Making a choice rather than accepting whatever comes your way builds character, resilience and focus. Without these foundations, the winds of change will be devastating.

Once you have found what inspires you and have developed the attitudes that kindle the desire to aspire to your dreams or goals, then perspiration is needed. All that is left is to just do it!

Journey back in time with us to the days when dairy

products were delivered by a milkman in a horse-drawn milk wagon. Lying in bed early in the morning you could hear the clip-clop of the horse as it moved slowly up the street. The milk wagon had a door on each side, located toward the front of the wagon which itself swayed from side to side adding the clinking of bottles hitting against each other in their racks to the familiar clip-clop sounds. The milkman would first step out one side of the wagon carrying the milk, eggs and butter to the customer's doorstep, would deposit the product, pick up empty bottles and the order for the next delivery and then re-enter the wagon to grab the products to be delivered to the house across the street, exiting out the opposite door.

This routine would go on with predictable rhythm until a new customer was added or an old customer deleted from the route. The horse had learned from repetition what was to be expected, how many stops would be made and where, and how long it would be until it could return to its stall and food. When there was a disruption to its routine, the horse refused to accept the change. You always knew when there was a difference in the route because you heard the milkman giving sharp orders to the horse for "whoa" or "git-up" as the case may be and could hear the slap of the reins on its back. On normal days he had no need to grab the reins, for a gentle command from time-to-time was all that was needed. But when there was a change he had to assume more responsibility to control the horse until the time came when it had accepted the change and no longer needed strong directions. Changing habits is much like getting that horse to recognize that the route had changed. The first day you do something different will be difficult. The second day will be as difficult. Every day for at least thirty days you will need to correct the "brain" as it tries to keep to the old route. Finally the day comes when it has learned the new route and, without your having to prod it, will automatically make the correct stops. A new habit has been established.

Perspiration means changing habits so that actions are congruent with inspired goals and desire. Otherwise, the old paradigm remains.

To go beyond paradigm is to experience a shift in perspective. Whenever there has been a paradigm shift in history (yours or the world's) the results have been revolutionary. There is one more attribute that is a necessary building block for mastering change. Let's begin with a general overview of our progress from thinking of the universe as mechanical to understanding it as a living organism.

Before Newton, people viewed the world as one in

which there was a God that made all the decisions. Any specific event, good or bad, was attributed to the actions of God. Around the time Newton proposed his scientific theories, people began to question that world view and began to believe that God had put into the universe a set of principles for mankind to discover and understand. Thus the dawn of the Newtonian age of mechanics where everything was set in a predictable and orderly pattern.

Around the time of Einstein people began to question a God and universe comprised of purely mechanical principles. With the dawn of the theories of relativity and wave mechanics, humans began to comprehend the relationships between living matter and discovered that the principles were taking on additional characteristics. Thus the current thinking of living systems which possesses a propensity to self-organize. Patterns and fractals found in living creatures and plants point to smaller building blocks which contain complete information of the whole. A hologram provides an example of this phenomena.

The first exposure one of us had to holograms took place in the late 1960's. Having been called down to one of the research labs at Northwestern University in Evanston, Illinois, to see the new holographic phenomenon, the central focus was a cloud of smoke in the middle of the room. On one side of the cloud was a glass plate on which there were moire patterns, reminiscent of the pattern seen on a rayon ribbon. A laser beam was then reflected through the glass plate and there in the haze of smoke was a three-dimensional object, a tea pot. Walking into the cloud of smoke and approaching the tea pot, it was possible to read on the bottom. "Made in England." By climbing up on a chair and looking down into the tea pot, the level of the tea could be seen. One day the glass plate was broken into several pieces. But the surprise was that when one of the pieces of the broken glass was put into the clamp and a laser beam reflected through it, it was found to contain the whole picture, not just a piece of the picture.

Developing the attribute of becoming a hologram creates the environment with you that will nurture your efforts toward fulfilling your true destiny. It is necessary to accept personally the challenge of becoming a hologram.

Becoming a hologram requires placing within the design on the glass plate of your life the necessary values, skills, knowledge and passion to define who and what you are in all situations. Therefore, your hologram contains all there is about you and does not vary from personal to professional life.

As an employee you will add to your hologram the knowledge of all aspects of the business in which you are involved which includes awareness of your customers, vendors, competitors and the marketplace in general as well as the changes taking place in the world.

If you are a business owner and not an employee, you most likely assume that since you are the hologram of the organization, this attribute doesn't apply to you. You couldn't be farther from the truth. Your responsibility is to fervently assist in any and all ways to develop the hologram for success within your employees. You must continually remind them of the purpose of the organization, encourage them in their present activities or mission and, above all, you must clearly define the vision of the future. Each employee may have their own individually developed hologram of *how* to achieve the vision, but with the shared common knowledge of the past, understanding of present expectations and desire to reach the future, each employee will understand *why* the formula is necessary for success.

We are keenly aware of business owners who, as individuals, are extremely successful. Unfortunately in their quest to assure their business meets their goals, they retain all control for decision-making and planning. As a result when they are absent from the business, everything comes to a halt for no one else can or desires to make a decision on their own causing the business to be compromised. Many otherwise successful businesses have failed because the owner or leader abdicated their responsibility to share this formula for success.

We are also keenly aware of those businesses where the owner has taken the time to instill within each employee a full understanding of the mission and vision for the business. The business runs as well when the owner is absent as when the owner is present. Surrounded by holographic employees, these owners are free to cultivate relationships necessary to maintain success in the future and enjoy the luxury of trusting those around them to reach the shared vision.

Inspiration, aspiration and perspiration. The Change Master will eagerly develop these attributes thereby creating a future that will make the most of their talent, interests and energy. They will choose to venture beyond their paradigm

problem (prôb-lem) *n.* a question or situation that presents uncertainty, perplexity or difficulty

CHAPTER EIGHT

MORE THAN A PROBLEM

Problems are a given in life. Everyone has experience dealing with problems. In spite of these facts, very few problems have been successfully eliminated. Perhaps that is because too often past practice is the basis of all attempts to solve problems. Once a solution has been implemented it becomes the action of choice in solving all future problems.

R. Buckminster Fuller once wrote on this subject as follows:

> *I am enthusiastic over humanity's extraordinary and sometimes very timely ingenuities. If you are in a shipwreck and all the boats are gone, a piano top buoyant enough to keep*

you afloat may come along and make a fortuitous life preserver. This is not to say, though, that the best way to design a life preserver is in the form of a piano top. I think that we are clinging to a great many piano tops in accepting yesterday's fortuitous contrivings as constituting the only means for solving a given problem.

Lee Iacocca, during a recent presentation we attended, emphasized that businesses have not yet recognized the difference between managing problems and solving problems. His observation was that when a problem is managed, the focus is on gaining control and making things better. In the process of allocating resources to this activity, the underlying problem is not addressed and will re-surface in spite of management's intervention.

Business schools and mentors have taught us that there are three steps to treating problems: absolution, resolution and solution. These are all familiar approaches.

A problem is absolved by ignoring it, hoping it will go away or solve itself.

A problem is resolved by implementing a clinical approach employing trial and error, experience and common sense. The problem is resolved with an outcome that is good enough that it will satisfy. The cause of the problem is not identified and so it should be no surprise that the organization returns to its previous state.

A problem is solved by taking a research approach relying on experimentation and quantitative analysis. In this process we seek an outcome that optimizes by giving the best possible outcome. In reality the problem is not being solved, it is being managed, or temporarily fixed.

An example of taking the approach of solving problems occurred in an early implementation program of a newly installed mainframe computer some years ago. The new computer kept crashing, but the pressure to make it work was great. To make sure the group was fixing problems as they arose, there were regularly scheduled morning meetings to go over the latest problem and seek solutions. Through this process, the programmers became so efficient at fixing problems as they occurred, that soon solutions were brought to the meeting rather than problems. Because of the efficiency of the group in fixing problems, the programs were not re-written. It was decided that it would take too much time to re-write the program since the solutions were working well. As new versions of the software were supplied by the vendor, more time was required to be devoted to making modifications to the new versions to accommodate the solutions that had been "tacked on" to fix past problems.

Early in the process, no one had taken the time to look to the future. It was determined that by managing or fixing the problems the group was only using 10% of their resources which was not bad. To stop and re-write the program would take about two thousand hours. It seemed quite appropriate to make those small modifications. After three or four years, however, far more than two thousand hours had been spent in making up for the deficiencies caused by the solutions.

Immanuel Kant, the great philosopher, was in the habit of keeping paper and pen on his bedside table. Often he would wake up in the middle of the night and jot down a thought or idea. Then he would go back to sleep. One morning he awoke convinced he had discovered the answer to a question that had puzzled him for months. While dreaming, he had a dazzling insight that seemed to break the mental logjam. He seized the paper on his bedside table in eager anticipation. There he found the words: *Think in different terms.*

By thinking in different terms, perhaps we can come to realize there is a fourth way to deal with a problem

that goes beyond solution. It is dissolution. To dissolve a problem is to eliminate it. The Change Master does not get caught up in managing or solving problems. They seek to eliminate the problem.
Before we embark on the secret to eliminating problems, we'd like to offer a few tools that will allow you to begin thinking in different terms when it comes to addressing problems.

The first tool is to view the whole system, not just the area in which the problem is occurring.

A textbook example of what it means to view the whole system is found in a problem a city was experiencing in its public transportation department. The problem existed between bus drivers and conductors. Each bus had a driver and conductor. The driver received an incentive for keeping on schedule. The conductor was responsible for collecting fares from passengers, issuing receipts for the various stops and then collecting those receipts when the passenger got off, checking them to see that the correct fare had been paid. Conductors received an incentive for making fewer errors. It is the conductor that signals the driver when the bus is ready to move on after each stop. During rush hours, conductors would let passengers board without collecting the fares and then try to collect them between stops. Because of crowded conditions on the bus they could not always return to the bus door to signal the driver to move on. This caused the driver to run late which meant he lost his incentive. As a result cooperation between drivers and conductors ceased and altercations between the factions sometimes approached violent outbursts. Management, looking at the problem, suggested that incentives be shared equally between conductors and drivers, or that incentives be eliminated altogether and that late schedules be made acceptable. Management's suggestions were vehemently rejected by the conductors and drivers.

Finally, someone looked at the whole system and sought a way to eliminate the problem. The result was that during rush hours the conductors were moved off the buses and placed at the stops. Under this system conductors collected fares from people while they were waiting for the buses, were at the door to signal the driver when he could move on, and could check the receipts of those leaving the bus. During non-rush hours, the conductors returned to the buses. The problem ceased to exist.

A second tool is to recognize that a problem may not be singular in nature. There may be more than one variable involved.

Any auto mechanic, professional or backyard variety, will attest to the pitfalls of this view of problem solving. What appears to be a battery that isn't working properly is actually *both* the battery and an additional problem with the ignition system. Using the hit and miss approach, eventually all contributing factors will have been isolated and repaired.

One way to sort out multiple variables is to focus on one issue at a time to heighten awareness. For example, when walking through your home, office or manufacturing facility, listen for unfamiliar sounds and trace their origin. Another day focus only on cracks in the walls or ceilings. Another day look from a different perspective, for example from the roof or the catwalk or the top of the stairs. Enter the room or facility as a customer, guest, vendor, new employee, or designer. You will discover information that will allow you to ask the questions that lead to problem elimination as well as discover problems about to happen.

A third tool is to recognize that there is no "one way" to solve a problem. What worked in the past may not be relevant to the present, whether in the same or modified format. To begin with, if the problem has resurfaced, then the past solution may have been just that -- a solution rather than the elimination of the problem. To blindly apply past practice to the current issue represents a refusal to think in a different way. We are reminded of a game of questions which is a family favorite. It has the following instruction: "Every question is a trick question." Likewise every problem should be viewed as a trick problem where the solution that immediately springs to mind may not address the specifics of the issue at hand.

An example is found in the familiar story of the young wife that was preparing the holiday ham when her husband entered the kitchen. She was having trouble cutting off the end of the ham and asked for his help. While engaged in the process, he asked his wife why she was cutting off the end of the ham. The answer was that it was the way her mother had taught her. The next day at the table the subject came up for discussion. The mother indicated that she had always cut off the end of the ham because that is how *her* mother had prepared the ham. When the grandmother was questioned about the process she replied that the only reason she cut off the end of the ham was because unless she did, it wouldn't fit in the pan.

Looking for new approaches rather than always applying the old way allows you to rise above the rest of the crowd.

A fourth tool is to involve others in the process of seeking to eliminate a problem. In today's fast paced world, no one person can be expected to know everything. By seeking input from those who have a stake in the problem, a new way of thinking will prevail and the odds of eliminating the problem rather than merely solving the problem are greatly increased.

An ancient Persian story tells of a father who has four sons. He has property in a far off place in the middle of which sits a beautiful and bountiful fig tree. The father sends his sons, one at a time, to bring back a report of how the tree is doing. The first son is dispatched at the height of spring and comes back saying that there is not much to the tree, for there are only small growths at the end of the twigs. The second son is dispatched in the summer and brings back a much different report. He sees the tree as best suited for a comfortable shady respite to escape from the sun. The third son is dispatched in the fall and comes back with baskets of delicious figs and believes that more trees should be planted. The fourth son is dispatched in the winter season. He finds bare branches and a tree that appears to be dead. He reports to his father that the tree is dead and needs to be chopped down. Four sons with four reports, all of which are accurate, yet none alone giving the complete picture. By including others when seeking to dissolve a problem, different viewpoints and expertise are brought to the issue which increases awareness and sensitivity to all facets presented by the problem.

Why include the issue of problems in a book about change? Because in these times of unprecedented change, we are assured of uncertainty and new challenges. Diverting valuable time, energy and resources to deal with recurring problems in addition to the new challenges that are being continually thrown our way can mean the difference between success and failure.

Let's return to that piano top that is serving as a life preserver. It certainly represents an immediate and creative solution to a critical need, but expecting it to be the answer to all critical needs is a bit far-fetched. Yet this is what happens time and time again, because individuals and organizations neglect to take the second step.

Whether at the outset or after being worn down from repetition, the majority of individuals, in attempting to successfully grapple with a problem, will eventually seek to find the root of the issue. Once convinced that this has been achieved, the plan is implemented and attention is turned elsewhere. Because the individual is convinced they have a good plan and sincerely believes they had identified the root of the issue, they are surprised when the problem creeps up again in the same or slightly different format. What went wrong, they wonder. However, as they feel comfortable with the plan of action, it is implemented again, perhaps more forcefully. Each time they get better at the implementation, but the same or new problems keep cropping up. How can we minimize this pattern of recurring problems?

The answer lies in taking the second step. The second step is taking a look at your plan of action for eliminating the problem and then projecting into the future to discover the problems the implementation of the solution will cause. The second-level problems are the ones that need to be addressed.

Buckminster Fuller in developing his geodesic dome

found that there were three parts to any situation. First was the force and last was the result. In between lies a space. We have taken the liberty to modify his observation and apply it to eliminating problems. Every issue (problem) has a cause (Buckminster's "force") and effect (Buckminster's "result"), but lying between the cause and effect is a path which can be used for leverage. The concept can be illustrated as follows:

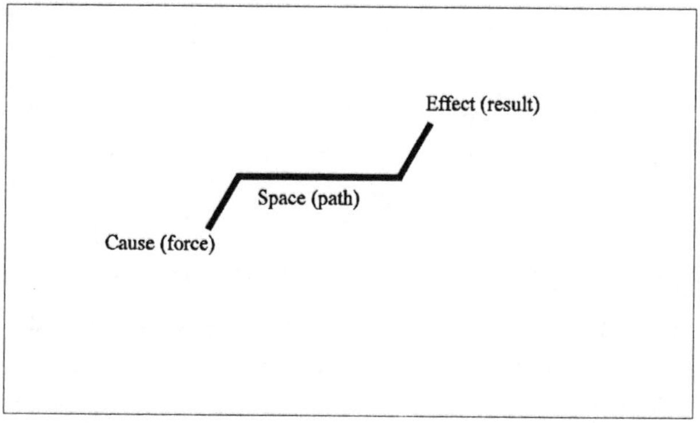

Figure 8.1

The cause, or force, leads to an effect, or result. But the space between cause and effect contains the path which the problem takes. We invariably turn our attention to the result and seek to minimize or eliminate what we find. In the process of seeking the fix or solution, the path is totally overlooked. It is the path which contains the leverage to the next problem.

How do you take the second step? There are three approaches when applied, alone or together, will assist you in locating the path between the cause and effect and allow you to eliminate the problem at hand as well as minimize or eliminate the problem the solution will bring about. These steps are: (1) Ask the right questions; (2) use both your right and left brain; and (3) step outside the problem.

Some of the right questions to ask are: "If I do this, what could possibly go wrong?" "If I don't do this, what will happen?" "When this solution is applied, what will need to be done next?" The answers to these and similar questions will save valuable time, resources and frustration.

By now most of us are acquainted with the left-brain, right-brain studies. These studies have shown that the left brain is primarily responsible for our verbal and logical thought processes whereas the right brain is the source of the spatial and nonverbal activities. Each individual has a propensity to favor one approach over the other. When approaching problems, attempt to engage the less familiar side of your brain to bring new insight to the issue. If you are verbal, then sketch out the problem to convey feelings and thoughts. If you are spatial and nonverbal, then talk aloud to yourself so you can "hear" the problem. While this may seem impossible, keep in mind that we often "cross-over" to the other side of our brain without even realizing it. Henri Matisse, the French artist, in replying to

Gertrude Stein's question of whether, when eating a tomato, he looked at it the way an artist would, stated:

> *"No, when I eat a tomato I look at it the way anyone else would. But when I paint a tomato, then I see it differently."*

Focus on using the less familiar method of applying your brain power to the issue and you will discover aspects that would otherwise be overlooked and will more likely ferret out additional ways to eliminate the problem.

Finally, step outside the problem. Disengage yourself from the issue and allow yourself to imagine floating above, around and below it to seek innovative approaches. Often while an organization or individual is in the midst of a problem they become caught up in the chaos and emotions of the issue and compromise or lose objectivity. By stepping outside the problem objectively and creativity can be regained.

Application of these three steps will bring forth both the absurd and real issues that then may result from a proposed solution. This information and awareness more often than not results in eliminating the current problem while minimizing or dissolving the next issue.

An example of what happens when the second step is overlooked took place when NASA constructed a massive building to house the early rockets that would launch man into space. The rockets and space capsule were to be assembled on site and a structure was necessary to protect them from the light rain showers Florida experiences almost daily, as is the case in most tropical environs. Engineers and architects spent many hours planning the structure, focusing on issues of structural strength, seeking appropriate materials, and drawing up plans. They solved the problems inherent in such a project and proceeded to construct the building to house the rockets and space capsule. However, they did not go the next step and ask questions beyond the physical attributes and integrity of the structure itself. They also did not attempt to apply the total brain or to step outside the issue. As a result they designed and constructed a building that was so big it created its own weather environment. The external heating of the roof of the building coupled with the inner air currents and height created a perfect atmosphere for small rain clouds to form and showers to occur inside the building, while the sun was shining outside.

Taking the second step will allow the Change Master the advantage of gaining time and eliminating unnecessary costs through the dissolution of problems. They will also recognize the paradox of change that occurs in dissolving problems. Just as taking the second step gives an edge to an organization, taking the third step is not as productive, at least at this time. Because of the impact of the speed and complexity of change, it is too difficult to accurately project beyond the second step.

Problems will continue to be a given in life. We can count on it. However, being aware of the secret of true problem-solving -- that is, thinking in new terms to dissolve problems -- the negative effects can be harnessed to our advantage and we will move beyond the piano top.

Childlike (chīld´līk) *adj.* Like a child, as in ingenuousness

CHAPTER NINE

BE A CHILD

This morning rushing into church being gently pushed ahead by a group of people trying to get out of gale-force winds and threatening rain clouds, I was caught up short by the sudden halting of all movement. The cause? A child, about three years old, who had suddenly stopped, squatted down in the middle of the doorway, oblivious to the onslaught of adults and any possible danger. He was squealing with great excitement, "Look, Mommy, see the caterpillar!"

A quick look around at the crowd hurrying to protect their clothes, hair styles and late schedules, exposed faces displaying irritation with the interruption rather than a shared excitement with the child's discovery. I couldn't help but wonder to myself, "what happens to us as adults that we rob ourselves of this joy of discovery?"

Perhaps it could rightfully be argued that a busy doorway to church just minutes before services is not the right time and place to explore the whimsical path of a fuzzy caterpillar. However, to fully participate in life it is necessary to recognize when the joy of the discovery of the moment cannot be postponed and must be explored. As Patricia Clafford noted: *the work will wait while you show the child the rainbow, but the rainbow won't wait while you do the work.*

We are not advocating being childish or immature. Those behaviors spring from being selfish and self-centered. On the other hand, we do speak boldly for the attribute of remaining childlike as a very effective method for mastering the ill effects of change.

There are four characteristics of a child that are of particular interest. The first is the child's delight in participating as an active partner with life. Second is their ability to see the world as it really is, rather than as others have defined it. Third is the child's unabashed imagination. Finally, there is their extremely high level of self-confidence and self-esteem. Believe it or not, cultivating each of these attributes will enable the adult to achieve mastery over change in their professional or personal life.

The first characteristic to be explored is that of

becoming a full participant in all life has to offer. A visit to a university Child Development clinic holds some clues. There an individual is allowed to sit in an observation booth and watch what goes on in the pre-school and kindergarten classes below. The academic challenge is to identify certain social and developmental phenomena, but the joy comes with watching children explore their world. The best times involve living creatures. Frogs, lizards, ant farms, puppies and fish are all fascinating to watch and try to understand. Much of the child's learning comes from direct experimentation and observation. They become caught up in the movements of the creature, how it reacts to their touch and voice, what it eats and how it sleeps. The most fundamental and simple attributes are exciting discoveries. For a child, the next best thing to observing animals is to find something in which to be fully involved, like finger painting, cookie making or dishing up ice cream sundaes. There is no preoccupation of concerns regarding getting dirty nor any preconceived idea of what should be expected. They go into the experience believing there really is more than one way to get finger paints onto paper or ice cream from a carton. They try their way, look around to see what others are doing and then either stick to their original approach, copy others or come up with something in between what the others are doing. The goal is to find what works for them.

The principle to be garnered from this attribute is that the object under a child's scrutiny has their full attention. They are caught up in the moment of discovery and curiosity. Nothing is ordinary or repetitious, *this* caterpillar is different from any other because it is the one they are watching at the moment. Then come the questions. Why? How? When? Is it always this way? When did I see something like this before? What will happen next?

Participating in life does not come as naturally for adults. Adults with their busy lifestyles and full calendars have taught themselves that it is frivolous to spend time on what appears to be unproductive matters. In the process they have relinquished a passion for living and the joy of discovering the unexplored facets of the ordinary. They have forgotten the lesson from their childhood that within the ordinary events of the day lie keys for understanding the future, developing new skills and attaining new insights.

Becoming a full participant in life is and will always be an option. On a recent television interview, a 70 year old man suffering from ALS, Lou Gehrig's disease, was discussing his impending death and deterioration of his physical body. His mind was sharp and he had surrounded himself with friends who would take time to sit and discuss many philosophical as well as ordinary topics. Everyone who came in contact with him had one particular observation, each stated in their own unique way, but all saying the same thing: He has become a true partner with life. He is more alive, more interested and interesting than in the sixty-five years that preceded this ailment. Best of all he has shown us that life holds fascination, magic and energy in the best of times and in the worst of times.

Another characteristic of participating in life is observing how the child celebrates what they have learned or accomplished. They are quick to show off what they have done and to seek appropriate praise from themselves and from others. But once they have celebrated, they move on to the next adventure, as though they have an innate understanding that there is still more to be discovered and no time should be lost.

As adults we tend to hang on to the moment of our accomplishment, sometimes for years, unwilling to move on too quickly to the next challenge. An extremely successful designer/architect that we know builds and renovates homes and offices in a most creative way. His work has been touted in many national publications and is readily recognized among his peers. He openly admits that he takes delight in the recognition, but says that the next project holds as much excitement and promise for success as his last. To stop too long to bask in the light of the current accomplishment would rob him of full participation in the next project.

Because of the rapid waves of change it is important to understand that while celebration is important, it can be counterproductive if everything stops at that point and there is no moving on to the next adventure.

You must make the choice to participate in life rather than just let life happen. Challenge yourself to find the joy and excitement of participating in the ordinary as well as the extraordinary.

The second characteristic of being childlike is to see the world as it really is rather than as others define it.

One of the stories that I am sure you heard as a child was *The Emperor's New Clothes.* As you recall the emperor sent for tailors to design for him a new set of clothes that would be better than anything he had ever possessed. The emperor was not known for his kindly manner and the tailors were keenly aware that if they did not produce an outstanding set of clothing they might not live to see next year. As the story unfolds the tailors present an imaginary set of clothes pretending to hold them up and describing them in great detail. Their story is so convincing that they soon have the emperor's court telling the same tale and making quite a fuss over the new outfit. The emperor, convinced that there must be something wrong with *his* eyes goes along with the crowd and likewise makes grand statements about the cleverness of his new tailors. To be sure everyone in his kingdom can experience first hand the sight of this extraordinary feat, he schedules a parade down the main street of the town. When the emperor strode naked through the streets all his subjects forced themselves to believe that he was splendidly clothed because they had been told that he wore his finest new clothing. It was a child who proclaimed in a loud voice, "But he doesn't have any clothes on at all!"

How many times as adults have we sat in a business meeting or on a committee and outwardly agreed with the rest of our companions on an issue or method when in our hearts we had that nagging feeling that there was something innately wrong with the decision, or that an important question may have been overlooked? How many times have we acted on that feeling at that meeting at that time?

During a psychology course at college, it was mandatory to take part in a minimum of three experiments being conducted by graduate students on social behavior. One such experiment involved a board with several lights and a switch. We were told that if we agreed with a certain statement we were to turn the switch on; if we disagreed we were to leave it in the off position. Each of the lights represented one of the other students who were located in other areas of the room out of our eyesight, so we could know how they were also answering the question. The question would be asked, we would decide on our answer and at the command would either turn the switch on or off. Then we would see how the others had "voted" on the topic. Once we had that information, we had an opportunity to change our answer. At first the board of lights showed a disparity in our answers. By the end of the evening, a "leader" had emerged and whenever that particular light came on others began to change their answers accordingly. Leader is in quotes for a reason. It was the experimenter who would say from time to time that the person with the green light was getting more of the answers correct or was responding better than the others. Soon everyone was doing what the green light was doing. Only after the experiment was over were we informed that the experimenter was the green light. By that time we had ceased listening to the questions and thinking for ourselves and had instead waited for the green light to decide the answer for us.

By neglecting to develop our ability to see the world as it is, we have made the choice to allow others to define it for us. The result is we end up following the green light. What a terrible surprise to learn that the green light had no relevance to the truth and instead was just a ploy to see how far we could be led down their path, fulfilling their agenda.

Do not relinquish the childlike characteristic of exploring the world to see it for what it really is.

The third characteristic is a child's imagination. We are speaking of imagination in terms of the process or power to form a mental picture of something.

The child in us is naive and innocent in the simplistic sense. A pillow case, a paper towel tube and an aluminum foil covered cardboard crown can transport a child into adventures untold. In their pretend times the world is transformed to new dimensions and objects take on new meanings. In their quest to become a dragon slayer, they imagine new uses for ordinary objects.

In a recent article in *Natural History* concerning the development of language, the author, Jared Diamond[1] pointed out that all inventions throughout history have basically spread in one of two basic ways. His example was the British battle cruisers in 1916 that were being blown out of the water by the Germans. The British wanted to develop battle ships that would be faster, believing that if they could outrun their enemies and be more maneuverable they could win the battles. Their naval designers came up with adding large turbine engines to the vessels to make them faster. The trade-off was to eliminate some of the armor. The blueprints were shared openly with their then allies, the Japanese who copied the blueprint. The Japanese navy had the same experience as the British when they encountered the American fleet in 1942 and saw their faster battle cruisers being blown out of the water.

The Germans, in 1905 stumbled on the fact the British were making their ships faster. They had caught the idea, but they didn't have the blueprint. Their naval designers were faced with developing their own blueprint and in so doing increased the size of the turbine engine, but kept the armor in place. In the end they had created superior vessels.

To be imaginative does not necessarily mean that one must be the creator of a process or idea. For the child the pillow case could become a cape, a bag to hold the treasures he claimed as a pirate, the challenge as he put both legs inside and tried to hop across a finish line in a race with others, or even a pillow case. We decide whether we will accept a blueprint as it is or whether we will add imagination to the formula and develop something unique for our own situation.

Don't be afraid to daydream and imagine. Therein may lie the key to redesign the effects of change to your advantage.

The final characteristic is the child's strong sense of self-confidence and self-esteem. Anyone who has been around a two or three year old will have experienced their strong-willed determination to "do it myself!" In their quest to experience something new, they are not thwarted by a sense of failing. They believe in themselves, their abilities and capabilities.

Thomas Edison displayed this childlike characteristic in his introduction of the phonograph in 1877. The first phonograph ever built was a cylinder on a shaft with a handle for turning the cylinder. There was a diaphragm at each end of the tinfoil wrapped cylinder so that when the soundwaves hit the diaphragms they would cause vibrations. A needle moving across the tinfoil would record different sounds by scratching grooves of different depths at it went along. The phonograph was Edison's invention; no one had ever made an attempt to record the human voice.

There were more skeptics than believers in the invention. First of all it was hard to believe that without some kind of trickery a machine could mimic a human voice. Second, even if it did work, there was no practical use for such an invention.

Nevertheless, in 1878 Edison was invited to bring his phonograph to the National Academy of Sciences in Washington D.C. President Rutherford B. Hayes had learned that Edison was in town and invited him to bring his invention to the White House. Edison complied and asked if the first lady, known as a very prim and proper woman, would be able to join them. According to historians, the President's wife was already in bed but willingly dressed and came down to join the group. The invention so fascinated the first family that they kept Edison up until the wee hours of the morning.

Edison next met with members of the Senate and House of Representatives. The meeting took place in the home of the famed Washington D.C. hostess, Gail Hamilton. Edison asked her to record a nursery rhyme. The phonograph repeated the lines and listeners were amazed by what they heard. At long last, the skeptics had been convinced that there was no magic involved and that the machine worked.

Edison believed in himself and in his invention. Later in life when asked what he thought was one of his greatest contributions, without hesitation he picked the phonograph. By then great voices like Enrico Caruso were being preserved for future generations. Other uses, such as for dictating business documents, were also being applied to the technology. Although earlier ridiculed and doubted, Edison never lost his self-confidence.

It is childish to be stubborn but childlike to believe in yourself and your ideas enough to pursue them. The child knows there are no failures, just set-backs full of lessons on how not to do something the next time.

There is a fine line between childish and childlike. Let us offer a secret to telling the difference.

Stop and think back to your childhood and to the special box that you kept hidden out of reach of brothers and sisters, mothers and fathers, and even your very best friend. In that box could be found the treasures that meant something to you, but not to anyone else. Others might laugh or ask too many questions. The catseye marble that always made you a winner, the birds nest that had held the first robins you followed from egg to flight, or a copy of your first poem. Whatever is in that treasure box contains your heart and soul, what is important to you, what you are passionate about and what you never want to forget. Take time to look in your treasure box right now. What is it that you are holding close to your heart, that you have decided defines the important moments of your life. These are the things for which you are passionate, these are the issues for which you have great feeling, these are the goals that give a sense of accomplishment. Within this treasure box lies the foundation of your childlike capabilities. Explore the box, mentally take the objects out one at a time and relish the memories, go beyond the physical object to the ideas and feelings and beliefs that have made them special. Then ask yourself, how many treasures am I finding today, or have I given up looking?

In February 1933, G. J. Mecherle, founder and first president of the State Farm Mutual Automobile Insurance Company wrote the following in his annual President's Message:

> *The purpose of life is to be happy; to give pleasure to others; and to enrich the world. If, in our desire to make a living, we forget to make a life, our success, counted in material wealth, is of small value. If our friendly association over a period of ten years*

has not enriched our lives by the constant contact of our associates, we cannot justly feel that we have attained the full, real measure of success, as there is nothing lasting either in thought or action which does not permeate and gather of the substance of the heart.

Even when you are behind schedule running in out of the weather, learn from the child in the doorway exploring the wonders of a caterpillar. Stop, stoop down and take delight in seeing the world through the child's eyes. Learn the joy of being childlike.

As a Change Master you will continually add to your treasure box as you hone the qualities of becoming an active partner in life, seeing the world as it really is, being imaginative and developing an appropriate level of self-confidence and self-esteem. Best of all you will recognize that if there is ever an environment in which a creature is enveloped in change, it is that which surrounds a child. Rather than fighting or bemoaning the changes and interruptions, the true child will find within the delight and joy of living at that moment.

[1]Blueprints, Bloody Ships and Borrowed Letters by Jared Diamond (*Natural History*, March 1995).

Relationship (ri-lā´-shən-ship) *n.* a logical or natural association between two or more things.

CHAPTER TEN

RELATIONSHIPS

How ironic that in an era where you can exist with little or no interaction with others, relationships are a key to survival.

Consider for a moment the impersonal nature of twentieth-century living. A phone call to many business establishments today means an immediate connection to the voice-mail system which will automatically transfer you through as many as five different departments resulting in a pre-recorded message that is meant to fulfill your needs. No actual human being is ever involved in the transaction. If you get lost in the system or have questions, you are advised to punch # and start all over. Even calls to personal friends often amounts to nothing more than leaving a message on their answering machine. Any time of the day or night you can stop by an ATM, punch in the right numbers and receive cash, transfer funds from one account to another, check your balance or make your mortgage payment. Some easy loans can be made over the telephone, using the numbers to punch in the information. Within twenty-four hours you receive a recorded message on your answering machine that advises you that the funds have been deposited to your account. If you are traveling, before leaving your hotel room, turn on the television, punch in prescribed numbers displayed on the screen by using the remote and you have completed your check-out.

As we are writing this book, one of the latest issues being discussed in social science circles, is the lack of honesty and respect shown for others on the computer networks. As individuals "hide" behind their clever on-line names, they can say anything in any manner while remaining anonymous. Is etiquette and regard for others in danger of disappearing in the process?

Businesses are buried in computer print-outs, focusing on the bottom line, and comparing data thrust into the public domain created by unknown analysts. It appears that whatever is in print takes on the aura of being absolutely true and questions are too easily put aside. Even in reviewing raw data, we often overlook the relationship of one area to another, one measurement to another.

Businesses that have thrust hundreds of people out of their organizations under the guise of down-sizing, right-sizing or re-engineering have discovered the bottom line results have been less than expected. Recent data reported in the *Wall Street Journal,* as well as many other publications, has shown that fewer than 20% of the businesses undergoing these changes have realized the projected results.

The common thread in this research is that relationships with employees, customers, and suppliers was never a part of the equation. Instead, these elements are treated as numbers to be tossed around in an equation that somehow is expected to portray the desired result. Take out three individuals at $50,000 annual salary each, plus benefits, and the bottom line savings is projected to be $195,000. Imagine the surprise of upper management that the savings is only $45,000 at the end of the year. What happened?

In a predictable, mechanical environment, this approach is adequate. In that environment you can be assured that two plus two will always equal four. Not only will the answer always be four but it will always be a four with the exact characteristics that occurred the last time you added two and two. Today, with living organisms and an environment that supports chaos, two plus two equals four is guaranteed to only work for accountants.

Recognizing relationships among vendors and customers, among individuals in various settings, or among the data we are analyzing, is what can make or break a business or individual. Relationships have always been important, but in today's environment they have become an invaluable asset.

Developing relationships, whether personal or professional, requires implementation of certain principles. These principles include the gift of time, commitment, and trust.

When the world is demanding that we move faster, absorb more information and make decisions immediately, it seems relationships have been left behind as one of those activities we will "get to one day." As has been said many times, no one on their death bed ever says, "I wish I had spent more time at the office."

In this new era time is a precious commodity. We will admit that "precious commodity" is an oxymoron. A "commodity" is something that is useful but usually plentiful and indistinguishable from other similar objects. Corn, soybeans, pork bellies, flour and sugar are often items that come quickly to mind. These items are fairly indistinguishable one from the other and can be traded easily. A person borrows a cup of sugar but usually doesn't go into great detail about describing exact qualities of the product. Sugar is sugar. On the other hand, something that is precious has high value or worth. A gem is precious or an heirloom is precious.

It appears quite correct to label time as a precious commodity. Everyone has the same twenty-four hours in a day and in that sense time is a commodity. However, the quality of the time, the use of the time and the fact that time can never be re-gained makes it precious. The question becomes, how do we allot the use of our precious commodity?

Usually in setting priorities for the day by putting items on our "things to do" list, there are two glaring omissions. The first is time spent with ourselves and the second is time spent in other relationships. Somehow it is expected these activities will miraculously fit themselves into our busy schedules.

Setting time aside to spend with yourself may, on the surface, appear to be the one thing on your schedule that can be fit in whenever convenient. Yet a common thread among individuals who have stood out in history and who are leading fully balanced and successful lives is that they find time each day, or at least several times each week, to nurture their mental and physical bodies.

On a recent flight from California to Oklahoma, the routing called for changing planes at the new Denver Airport. A Korean woman was getting off the plane and I noticed she was trying to get her bearings. I had overheard her say she, too, was going to Oklahoma City so I offered to guide her to the gate. Hurrying through the airport in an effort to make the connecting flight at the opposite end of the concourse, she made the remark that she found America a beautiful country, but Americans were too busy rushing around.

The stress caused by rushing around can be deadly. On the other hand, there are some types of stress that can be invigorating. Permitting yourself to take time to reflect and pull away from the demands of the day is mandatory for mastering change. Sometimes it means getting up a half hour earlier in the morning, turning television off an hour earlier in the evening, or finding a quiet place during lunch. Reflecting, writing in a journal and reading inspirational books will assist in bringing calm into your life and refreshing your mental capabilities. Surprisingly, you will eventually find in those calm moments that original thoughts and ideas will begin to bubble to the surface. Your relaxation will result in creativity and renewed stamina. Likewise it is necessary to take time each day, or at least in several sessions a week, to exercise the physical body. In addition to maintaining muscle tone and improving general health, you will increase your energy level and sense of well-being.

Investing time in yourself will contribute a return that will make continuing the practice very profitable.

It is equally important to spend time with others. Others is loosely defined as those close to you as well as those with whom you have a business or professional relationship. There are many people with whom we are acquainted, but very few that are given the gift of time.

In personal relationships the gift of time means setting aside all other cares to focus on the other individual. It means listening when appropriate, engaging in activities which you both enjoy, supporting in times of distress, and occasionally just quietly being there. Magazines and books are filled with real-life stories of relationships that were lost, built or restored based solely on spending time in the relationship.

In the professional realm it is important to recognize that in the past you were valuable to your organization when you added value to the product. Today you are valuable when you assist the customer in meeting their needs. You cannot have a clue to the customer's needs if you have not invested the time to get to know them, their business and the challenges they face. An investment of time spent in getting to know your customers will allow you to become a partner in eliminating their problems.

Relationships don't occur without an investment of time. It is important for you to recognize this fact and take the initiative and time to make it happen.

Once time has been set aside to develop relationships, it is necessary to commit to the relationship. We're not talking about the proverbial male-female issue of commitment. Instead the focus is on the attribute of commitment that involves following through with promises to yourself and others.

A recent article in *Reader's Digest* describes a time when a father had promised his son he would be at his soccer game after school. Things at the office were getting out of hand and making the school event was becoming less of a probability. The father remembered that he had promised his son he would be there and felt that he must honor that commitment. The work was important but by taking time out of his evening at home, he could still make the game and make the deadline for the report in the morning. It would take more effort and he would lose a lot of sleep. He packed everything into his briefcase and set out for the soccer field, arriving late. The first part of the game had been played and the young men were scattered during the rest period. Looking around the father found his son sitting off by himself. He was sure that the young man was upset by his being late and was rehearsing what he would tell him about why he had missed the first part of the game. But as he came upon his son, the boy looked up and excitedly said, "I knew you would be here. I have been saving my drink to share with you." There had never been a doubt that Dad would keep his promise. Commitment takes effort, but brings about rewards.

In the professional arena commitment means following through on the promises to complete a report on time, to begin or finish a project, to be where you are expected and to be prepared. It is supporting those around you, subordinate and boss. Commitment means that you can be depended on to deliver.

Commitment is more than shear determination and action. True commitment comes from the heart and is based in the healthy desire to please others by following the "golden rule" of treating them like you would like to be treated. It is a basic attitude of caring for others, putting yourself in their shoes and acting accordingly.

The final principle is that of trust. Notice that building relationships is an on-going process. You begin with a gift of time that allows you get to know another person or organization. Then you increase the value of that relationship by nurturing it with your commitment to follow through on your promises. Finally, as a result of these actions, a trust begins to build between the parties.

Trust is defined as a confident belief or faith in another. It is the strongest building block in the relationship, and, paradoxically, is the most fragile. When trust has entered the relationship, you have reached the point where you can be openly honest, share confidences and seek advice and insight without fear of negative consequences.

King Arthur and his Knights of the Round Table provide an example of how relationships evolve.

King Arthur began with an idea to gather a special group of knights that would share a vision and mission setting them apart from any other such collection of knights. The group would sit at a Round Table so that there was no "head" to the table meaning that each knight was as valuable as the next. The knights were selected to be part of the Round Table for the special attributes they individually brought to the group. Each would serve the group with their strengths, but none would be required to relinquish their individuality in the process. They would meet regularly to discuss their mission and shared vision. They would constantly hone their skills through tournaments. Above all, they would get to know each other and build a level of trust that would result in their willingness to die for one another.

Marie Curie, discussing her many contributions to science, is quoted as saying:

> *I persist in believing that the ideas that then guided us are the only ones which can lead to true social progress. We cannot hope to build a better world without improving the individual. Toward this end, each of us must work toward his own highest development, accepting at the same time his share of responsibility in the general life of humanity.*

We are each responsible for the relationships we elect to develop and for the ideas and ethics we share and implement. Relationships are primarily between individuals and to be healthy they cannot be one-sided. There is an implied responsibility that we accept when we enter into any relationship which is to commit ourselves to not only making the relationship better, but to assisting the other individual in becoming all they can become.

Time. Commitment. Trust. These principles are necessary for there to be a meaningful relationship. Yet there is another element that occurs and that involves the heart. Any relationship -- intimate, personal or professional -- involves the emotions and the result is synergistic. In other words, the relationship is greater than the sum of the parts. As living, diverse, activities, there are other subtle lessons a master of change will take away from this experience.

Relationships come and go depending on the time or need in one's life or business. Not all relationships are for a lifetime. Some relationships are severed because of loss. The loss can be a joyful one as when a child leaves for college or gets married. The child will always be yours, but the relationship has taken on new aspects and there is no turning back. Sometimes the loss is caused by a friend moving away, or a business associate being promoted to another position or location, or a change in our primary contact within our customer's organization. Sometimes the loss is permanent as in the death of one of the parties. A relationship that has been lovingly nurtured through time, commitment and trust may, if we so desire, continue to exist in some form or another, but we must accept the fact that it will be different from the past. As we learn to mourn the losses that will ultimately be experienced in many relationships, we gain the resilience to withstand the losses that will be found in the environment of change.

Change sweeps in and forever alters the landscape of our life or business. Sometimes the alteration is small, sometimes it is major. But there is no denying that it is no longer the same. If we become caught up in trying to restore the old landscape against all odds, then we never leave the stage of mourning that is destructive. We must learn that part of life involves loss. It is necessary in our personal and professional lives to acknowledge the loss and allow the proper amount of time to mourn. Then we must accept the fact that it is time to detach oneself from the old and attach to the new. It is necessary to develop the ability to withstand the stress of loss. Recognizing the phenomena will allow you to enjoy more fully current relationships, savor the best of those relationships, and understand that in living creatures the landscape and environment in which we exist does not remain the same forever. Learning the skill of attaching and detaching is important to mastering change.

As with King Arthur, relationships throughout our lives ultimately make up our own Round Table of knights. Some are still with us and some have gone before. They have each contributed some idea, action, gift or attribute that has assisted us in reaching our life goal. Likewise, we will have contributed something to them that will allow them to reach their visions and goals in life.

There is an old story of a potter who took a lump of clay. He gently kneaded it with his hands and then divided it into two equal lumps. It is said he made a statue of you and a statue of me. He then took the two statues and smashed them, making them once again into one lump of clay. Then he gently kneaded the clay with his hands and divided it into two equal lumps. He again made a statue of you and a statue of me. But the difference is that now there is some of me in you and some of you in me.

That is great description of what relationships are all

about. In spite of the technology of the times, it is vital to recognize the value of relationships. Businesses that have taken the initiative to build strong relationships with their customers, vendors, stockholders and employees are those who have reaped the benefits of the synergies created from these efforts. Likewise, individuals will also find efforts that are devoted to building relationships will be well rewarded.

The master of change will not shy away from the importance of relationships and in so doing will enjoy greater success and an enriched life. Relationships will give strength and stability during times of change and will assist the Change Master in accepting the process of mourning that leads to resilience. They have come to accept the fact that in spite of the ability to technologically exist with little or no interaction with others, survival depends on the existence of relationships.

valuable (val´yoo-e-bel) *adj.* Of great importance, use, or service.

CHAPTER ELEVEN

MY CHAPTER ON CHANGE

If you are hurriedly thumbing through this book, this last chapter may seem rather strange. It appears to have been left uncompleted. Indeed your observation is correct. However the chapter is incomplete because it is *your* chapter on change. No one can write what change means to you or what change(s) you are undergoing except yourself.

This chapter will become one of the most valuable in the entire book for it is your chapter-in-the-works that will ultimately assist you in recognizing and applying the principles of mastering change.

✧✧✧✧✧

✏ *Do you write in the margins of the book you are reading? Do you highlight or underline sentences or words or ideas? If not, then please break that habit right now and mark up this book! [If you are intimidated by a pen, then mark in pencil!]*

✧✧✧✧✧

Keep in mind that change is neither good nor bad in and of itself. Change does, however, manifest itself in everyone's life in some form or another. Remember, change is nothing more than something other than what was expected. With that in mind, list some of the changes that have taken place in your life this past month:

____

____

____

If you were honest, you were able to list several items. But, if you are reading this book, you survived! The first principle is to recognize change is constantly occuring around you and is nothing to be feared. Following are a few exercises that will assist you in recognizing and implementing principles for mastering change.

✧✧✧✧✧

Above all, a Change Master will strive to become metanoic. The root of this attribute comes from the Greek word, metanoia, which means to think in different ways. Mastering change begins with thinking differently. The following tools will assist you in beginning your journey.

Creating new ideas: Creativity begins with breaking out of your current habits. Let's get started on this three-step process. . . .

(1) Words. The first thing you need to do is go out and buy an inexpensive paperback dictionary that is easy to carry with you. Select at random two words every day. The first word you choose will be one that is familiar to you. [You will be surprised at how many words you thought you knew....but didn't!] Then choose a word that is not familiar to you. Learn how to pronounce the word, the meaning of the word, and the history of the word. The purpose is *not* to learn the new word to use in your daily conversations, but merely for the joy of learning and stretching your mind and imagination. This is the beginning of mind-stretching and this exercise will not stop for the rest of your life.

	Familiar Word	New Word
Day One:	____________	____________
Day Two:	____________	____________

Day Three: ____________ ____________

Day Four: ____________ ____________

Day Five: ____________ ____________

Day Six: ____________ ____________

Day Seven: ____________ ____________

After you have been doing this word exercise for a minimum of 21 days, then you are ready to move on to the next step.

(2) Ideas. Create an idea file. Re-read that sentence because it does not say to create a file of *your* ideas. [That will come later.] Start by keeping copies of ideas that you find in newspapers, magazines, books, or newsletters. Jot down ideas that you hear and slip them into the file as well. The purpose is *not* to necessarily find the right idea for a specific problem but to develop your skills in searching for ideas. Just accumulate the material.

Once a month sit down in a quiet place and pick up your idea file, read everything in the file and begin to look for similarities or trends. Sort the articles into piles which signify specific trends or that cover the same areas.

Pick up your spiral bound notebook (which you will keep as your "Idea Book") and begin to jot down your thoughts and ideas on each of the stacks. What are the trends? What are things I can use now? What confirms some actions that I have taken in the past? Where are the ideas taking me? How can I use some of the ideas? Keep asking questions to make the most of the material.

Now, take some of your best thoughts and ideas and begin to talk to others about the ideas to get their input and insight.

Once again, you have undertaken an activity that will continue for a lifetime.

The above two steps have been undertaken by many people in many different ways. But only about 10% of those who begin keep up the exercise. Once you have joined the 10% and have mastered this discipline, you are on the way to thinking in different ways. Now you are ready for the last step.

(3) Involvement. This is the beginning of awareness. You may have an interest in painting and have enjoyed

the museums, art history books and, perhaps, collecting artwork. But have you become involved and taken a class or started to do the activity yourself?

Becoming involved means that you don't just watch a sport or activity, you become a player or coach. You don't just read about an activity, you actually do the activity. True understanding and awareness comes when you are involved in something.

It is not necessary to become an expert or devote all your time to involvement in any area. For example, you may decide to jump out of a plane -- you only need to do it once.

Take time now, assume no restrictions, and list some of the things you would like to experience first hand:

____

____

____

Prioritize the list according to your interests and set a goal for when you will begin to become involved in that activity.

The most important promise you will ever make is to yourself. Psychologists tell us that when we write something down we are more apt to remember and do whatever it is that we've committed to words. Make a written promise to yourself now...we'll give you a start on the pledge:

I, ____________, promise myself that by ________,

19__, I will begin to do ________________________

____.

Now, just do it! Keep a diary of the preparations, the experience and what you observed or learned that you didn't expect when you started.

Perhaps you will undertake something new each year, or perhaps you will devote two years to preparing and doing the activity. Each exercise is up to you. But once you have become involved in one activity, don't stop there. Chose another and treat yourself to the same experience.

The purpose of the above, long-term exercise is to gain awareness of you, your surroundings and the world. By undertaking these experiences you will see things around you in new ways, you will have more interesting conversations, you will search for new meanings and relationships.

✧✧✧✧✧

Sometimes it is necessary to see things differently, as well as think differently. The following will assist you in this shift of perspective.

Sit in your chair and think about a favorite room or place other than where you are now. Make a list of all the things you can remember from that familiar place.

____________________	____________________
____________________	____________________
____________________	____________________
____________________	____________________
____________________	____________________
____________________	____________________

Now go to that place and write down all the things that are there but are not on your list:

Think of baking cookies or taking a trip. Now walk through the process ***backwards***, listing all the steps:

✧✧✧✧✧

One who is able to master change has risked doing the impossible. Drawing is something that is impossible for many individuals. You may be surprised at how easy it is to do the impossible.

Get a pencil (erasers are not necessary) and let's begin:

Cover the bottom half of the page and draw the following picture in the box on the right :

Now the picture has been placed upside down. Cover the top half of the page and draw the picture in the empty box on the right .

Did you find it easier to draw with the picture upside down? What did you do differently when you drew the picture upside down?

____

____

____

____

✧✧✧✧✧

Get a box. It can be as big or as small as you desire and can be ornate or plain. Put the box in a place where you can easily see it and gain access to it. Over the next month, put a representation of everything that you have treasured with your time and energy into that box. At the end of the month, sit down in a quiet place and look at the contents.

My box includes:

____________________ ____________________

____________________ ____________________

Now in your imagination, think back over your life and list those things that you would have put in your box:

What do the contents of your boxes tell you about yourself? What surprised you? What caused you to laugh? Did you miss something in your box?

Notes on what I put in my box:

____

____

✧✧✧✧✧

Notes from my reading: ____________________

____

____

____

____

____

____

✧✧✧✧✧

Seeing and thinking differently *is* important to mastering change.

A mutual acquaintance, Robert Baker, one of the principals of Applied Intelligence Group, Inc. tells of his first parachute jump. He took the jump because he wanted to conquer his fear of heights and experience parachuting. He was fortunate enough to have as his instructor one of the instructors who jumps and teaches with the Air Force's competition jump team. Just before getting on the plane, the instructor grabbed Bob and, yelling over the noise of the plane's engines, began to shout out last minute instructions. Holding on to Bob with both hands, shaking him to assure he had his full attention, the instructor began yelling reminders. At three thousand feet Bob needed to pull the ripcord to release the main parachute. If it didn't open, then at two thousand feet Bob was to pull the ripcord to release the back-up chute. If that chute didn't open, at one thousand feet he was to "pull everything."

Bob wanted to know more about that last instruction -- "pull everything." The instructor shouted that too many people hit the ground yanking on their parachute harness, having mistaken the harness for the ripcord. By pulling at *all* cords and straps, Bob would be more apt to pull the right cord and release the parachute.

"I've got it!" Bob yelled back, nodding his head and giving the thumbs up sign, "But, tell me one more thing. How much time do I have to get my chute out between one thousand feet and the ground?"

Without blinking an eye, the instructor shouted the answer, "The rest of your life."

When you are surrounded by chaos, stress and change, it is not uncommon to hang on to the harness of the past, refusing to let go. By mastering the principles described in this book, you will find that even when you arrive at one thousand feet with a parachute that has not yet opened, you will have attained the knowledge and skills necessary to overcome the negative effects of change. In the process, you will have gained the "rest of your life."

Reference Material

Barker, Joel Arthur. *Discovering the Future: the business of Paradigms* (ILI Press, Lake Elmo, Minnesota) 1989.

Belasco, James A. Ph.D. *Teaching the Elephant to Dance: Empowering Change in Your Organization* (Crown Publishers, Inc., New York, New York) 1990.

Block, Peter. *Stewardship: Choosing Service Over Self-Interest* (Berrett-Koehler Publishers, San Francisco, California) 1993.

Board Room Reports. (Boardroom Reports, Inc., New York, New York).

Boorstin, Daniel J. *The Discoverers: A History of Man's Search to Know His World and Himself* (Vintage Books, New York, New York) 1983.

Bottom Line Personal (Boardroom Reports, Inc., New York, New York).

BusinessWeek. (McGraw-Hill Publishing, New York, New York.)

Canfield, Jack and Hansen, Mark Victor. *Chicken Soup for the Soul: 101 Stories to Open the Heart and Rekindle the Spirit* (Health Communications, Inc., Deerfield Beach, Florida) 1993.

Collins, James C. and Porras, Jerry I. *Built to Last: Successful Habits of Visionary Companies* (Harper Business, New York, New York) 1994.

Conner, Daryl R. *Managing at the Speed of Change: How Resilient Managers Succeed and Prosper Where Others Fail* (Villard Books, New York, New York) 1993.

Covey, Stephen R. *Principle-Centered Leadership* (Summit Books, New York, New York) 1991.

Covey, Stephen R. *The 7 Habits of Highly Effective People* (Simon & Schuster, New York, New York) 1989.

Crosby, Philip B. *Quality is Free* (A Mentor Book/New American Library, New York, New York) 1979.

Discover. (Disney Magazines, Palm Coast, Florida).

Drucker, Peter F. *Managing for the Future: The 1990s and Beyond* (Truman Talley Books/Dutton, New York, New York) 1992.

Edwards, Betty. *Drawing on the Right Side of the Brain.* (J. P. Tarcher, Inc., Los Angeles). 1979.

Forbes. (Forbes, Inc., New York, New York).

Frankl, Viktor E. *Man's Search for Meaning* (A Washington Square Press Publication of Pocket Books, New York, New York) revised and updated, 1984.

Fuller, R. Buckminster. *Operating Manual for Spaceship Earth* (Pocket Books, New York, New York). 1970

Gleick, James. *Chaos: Making a New Science* (Penguin Books, New York, New York) 1987.

Harrison, Allen F. and Bramson, Robert M. Ph.D. *The Art of Thinking* (Berkley Book/Doubleday & Company, Inc. New York, New York) 1982.

Hawking, Stephen. *A Brief History of Time* (Bantam Books, New York, New York) 1988.

Hawking, Stephen. *Black Holes and Baby Universes and other Essays* (Bantam Books, New York, New York) 1993.

Industry Week. (Penton Publishing, Inc., Cleveland, Ohio).

Landrum, Gene N. *Profiles of Genius: Thirteen Creative Men Who Changed the World* (Prometheus

Books, Buffalo, New York) 1993.

Newman, James W. *The World of Mathematics, Volumes 1-4.* (Simon and Schuster, New York, New York) 1956.

Olesen, Erik. *12 Steps to Mastering the Winds of Change: Peak Performers Reveal How to stay on Top in Times of Turmoil* (Rawson Associates, New York, New York) 1993.

Popcorn, Faith. *The Popcorn Report* (A Currency Book, published by Doubleday, New York, New York) 1991.

Success. (Success Partners, New York, New York).

Tichy, Noel. M. and Sherman, Stratford. *Control Your Destiny or Someone Else Will* (Currency Publications/Doubleday, New York, New York) 1993.

Tucker, Robert B. *Managing the Future: 10 Driving Forces of Change for the '90s* (G. P. Putnam's Sons, New York, New York) 1991.

Twain, Mark. *Adventures of Huckleberry Finn.* (Chelsea House) 1990.

Walton, Sam (with John Huey). *Sam Walton, Made in America, My Story* (Bantam Doubleday Dell

Publishing Group, Inc., New York, New York) 1992.

Wheatley, Margaret J. *Leadership and the New Science: Learning about Organization from an Orderly Universe.* (Berrett-Koehler Publishers, San Francisco, California) 1992.

Zukav, Gary. *The Dancing Wu Li Masters: An Overview of the New Physics* (Bantum Books, New York, New York) 1979.

About the Authors

Charles I. Merrick

Charles has over 30 years experience in business of which over 15 has been spent as a corporate executive, including CFO, in Fortune 500 companies. He was Chairman, CEO and owner of his own Fortune 1000 manufacturing business. This start-up business attained $260 million in domestic and export sales in less than three years. He also has extensive financial, industrial engineering, information systems and product design experience.

Kay Hunley Titchenal

Kay has over 25 years experience in both the public and private sector of manufacturing and service provider organizations. During her career she has assisted several entrepreneurs in successfully launching their businesses. She has experience in law, finance, human resources, public relations, construction site management, property management and food and nutrition.

Other notes. . .

Together Charles and Kay offer a background of solid experience in business and training.

They have successfully implemented self-directed teams and quality improvement processes in their own businesses In addition they have also successfully re-engineered corporate cultures and processes in existing businesses.

Ordering Information

If you would like to order additional copies of ***Change Master: Principles for Mastering Change***, you may contact the publisher at the following address:

Candlewick Square Publishing, Inc.
P. O. Box 93
Edmond, OK 73083-0093
(405) 359-8030

Copies are $12.95 each plus $3.00 for shipping and handling. Please send check or money order, payable to Candlewick Square Publishing, Inc., with your request. [Oklahoma residents, please add sales tax.]

Discount rates are available for 10 or more copies shipped to one address. Please write or call for additional information.